from science & religion to God

A narrative of Mary Baker Eddy's *Science and Health*

By Cheryl Petersen

www.HealingScienceToday.com

ISBN: 978-0-9795454-5-0

Neutrino Publishing

CONTENTS

Preface

I discover something new each day. Without science and religion, my discoveries could be very mysterious. But, I've also discovered something else very important.

Mysteries remain, if I get stuck in the thinking that science and religion are the sources of truth. Science and religion are not sources, they are methods, approaches, or practices.

Final truths are not found in science or religion. We find truth only in what I call, God, Truth with a capital T, the source and power behind discovery.

We may know our field of science or we may know our religion, but the minute we think we know truth, we stopped knowing truth, because Truth constantly reveals itself due to its infinite nature. *From science & religion to God* is a strong appeal to keep all methods of research useful by keeping them secondary to truth.

Focusing on God, we can capture fresh views of science and religion.

There is nothing new to this system of surrendering to Truth and further expanding our minds and possibilities. It brings healing to ourselves, our neighbors, and our earth because it involves love.

Truth and Love are one. Basically indefinable, but we know them when true love removes fear.

Truth causes us to be honest and care for ourselves and the environment. Love causes us to better ourselves, to fight for and share in a practical, meaningful life. We eventually realize that the consciousness of love is the only asset worth taking with us whether we move, change our image, or die.

Neither science nor religion have a complete understanding of everything. Arguing for one or the other doesn't bring understanding. So, with, *from science & religion to God,* we can contemplate a useful interpretation of God as a force that allows us to stop struggling.

We don't need to "change" bad into good, or lack into abundance, or sickness into health. Said in another way, we don't need to change darkness into light, but can discover how we are one with the light that naturally displaces the darkness.

The ideas in this book are thought based, rather than time- or thing-based. They discuss the practice of divine metaphysical healing.

From science & religion to God is a narrative based on a book written in the 19th century by Mary Baker Eddy, a person who also discovered the force of God and genuinely practiced this system of metaphysical healing successfully.

In the 19th century Mrs. Eddy defined this system as Christian Science. The word Science, capitalized, was applied to Christianity to exalt its meaning from creed and theory to deed and practice.

Subjects in this book encompass everyday life, touching on traditions, relationships, alternative healing, mind-power, the body, science, and religion. Near the end of the book is the chapter, *Study Guide,* with a Q&A section. The last chapter, *Glossary,* explains words and terms used.

You can start reading wherever it feels fitting. The message boils down to one sentence, written by Eddy long ago, "All is infinite Mind and its infinite manifestation."

The ideas in *from science & religion to God* explore a tremendous spiritual study, open to everyone, no matter what your background.

Cheryl

Traditions: Prayer, Communion, Marriage

Why then 'tis none to you; for there is nothing either good or bad, but thinking makes it so.[1]

Traditions can be healthy. They can be used to advance spiritual good. We have an example of this in the Bible, when Jesus dealt with the tradition of baptism.

Jesus came to John the Baptist, at the River Jordan, to be baptized. John resisted. He felt Jesus should baptize him instead. Jesus said, "Let it be so now, for thus it is fitting for us to fulfill all righteousness."[2]

At this point, baptism became more meaningful. It became a mindful experience. John or Jesus weren't the primary figures, God was. John and Jesus embraced humility and acknowledged a love and reverence for a Higher Power.

The event in turn was marked with peace and a powerful message from Spirit. "And when Jesus was baptized, immediately he went up from the water, and behold, the heavens were opened to him, and he saw the Spirit of God descending like a dove and coming to rest on him; and behold, a voice from

---

[1] *Hamlet Act 2, scene 2.* William Shakespeare (1564-1616), playwright and poet.
[2] Matthew 3:15

heaven said, 'This is my beloved Son, with whom I am well pleased.'"[3]

Rituals are unavoidable. We eat, we go to jobs, we participate in ceremonies, and we bend to hierarchies. As long as traditions don't become ego trips or mechanical nonsense, a higher ideal can infuse these practices with holy purposes.

Prayer

Prayer is the faith that all things positive and good are possible to God. Fed by selfless love, faith grows into spiritual understanding and reveals remarkable experiences.

God's work is done. We reflect the doing. The doing is not busy work reacting to our own personal desires or the world's demands, but a logical, spiritual, helpful, brave response to God's work—a prayer.

Thoughts are prayers. Desires are prayers. Sometimes these thoughts and desires are sketchy, but God can be trusted to clarify our prayers.

We may desire more righteousness, but is it a desire to be right with God, or to be right in the eyes of human beings? The motives for prayer will be exposed. You can't hide ulterior motives.

---

[3] Matthew 3:16-17; Mark 1:10-11; Luke 3:22; John 1:32-34

2

Healing prayer doesn't try to change God, because God is unchanging wisdom and Life. Prayer instead adapts us to wisdom and Life.

God already knows what we need. We are never telling God something new. Asking God for something, no matter how passionate we sound, doesn't guarantee satisfaction. Humility is necessary. Not humiliation, but humility.

Don't acquire the habit of pleading with God, as though God is a human being with a brain that can be triggered into action. It is a mistake to think prayer coaxes the divine Being into reality. God's universe is alive and well—synchronized with consciousness now. Spiritual being is intact.

God is divine Mind, intelligence, the all-knowing. Trying to give information to God is misleading. Sincerity in prayer brings us closer to the source of all existence and blessedness.

Wordy prayers have not proven reliable. Long-winded prayers take detours into unrealistic terrain, making promises they can't keep. Human beings are easily distracted. They are incapable of telling God what to do.

The wisdom of divine Mind can't be misled.

As we reflect the "altogether lovely,"[4] we are conscious of the image and likeness of God. This

---

[4] Song of Solomon 5:16, KJV

task of reflection is no small undertaking and demands total commitment of thought, energy, and desire.

Prayer must be kept modest and open to new ideas. Our understanding of God continues to grow because God is infinite. One shouldn't tell God, and everyone else, how to think and act. Dismiss the holier-than-thou attitudes that often taint prayer.

Being grateful is an important rule; however, being grateful for material wealth and physical health is different from being grateful for spiritual qualities sustained by Life, Truth, and Love. Gratitude for honesty, humility, and hard work, while we *live* the honesty, humility, and perseverance is powerful.

The prayer for grace is shown in courage, forbearance, love, and good deeds.

Silent prayer, spiritual awareness, and obedience come with the grace of Love. We are worthy of Love's grace. We can be patient with ourselves and with others, because in this complicated world most of us are rookies at internalizing the divine character.

Not only is it difficult to understand a God we can't physically see or control, but we've also been hardwired to materialize our prayers by repeating them out loud ad nauseam. Too much repetition disallows us from working out the next rule.

Mistakes are made every day. Quite often we are sorry especially for the mistakes that hurt other people or the environment. The remorse leads us to self-help books and support groups in an effort to reform. Then comes the hard part—when we have to face, admit, and figure out how not to repeat the hurtful, fearful, stupid thoughts and behaviors. We have to figure out how to reform.

Reformation is confusing because religious cultures emphasize superficial professions as if we confess our sins or believe in a Savior that we are thereby made free. But, mere confession and belief don't reform us.

Reformation is also problematic because societal cultures enforce civil laws that identify reformation with recompenses. If we break a civil law, we are required to pay a fine or do the time; however, neither action reforms or stops us from again breaking laws.

Reform comes when bad thoughts and behaviors are destroyed by good. Reform comes by a shift in thought and reasoning. We learn that egotistical, dim, greedy thoughts suffer and self-destruct and we want no part in them, so much so that they are dismissed from our psyches. We reason from the standpoint that God isn't, and never was, influenced by bad thoughts and a good God is our influence. We learn to lean on God and be re-formed by spiritual thoughts.

Reformation isn't the same as morphing from the physical to the spiritual, from bad to good. We rather see the opportunity to shine our God-given light. As we shine the light of pure goodness, we feel re-formed.

Darkness is not turned into light. Light shines and the darkness is naturally displaced. This rule is also effective when praying for physical healing to a God that created and only reveals health. Realize that a sick body isn't made better, but sickness is dissolved as health and healing are admitted.

Don't be fooled by the concept of sin. We weren't born sinners. We do, however, commonly believe we were born human beings, inadequate mortals vulnerable to what has been labeled sin. When we are not in tune with our spiritual beingness we make mistakes—we sin. Unless the mistake-causing thought is destroyed, it will continue to cause suffering.

It is vain to believe sloppy or unfinished mental work will be excused. In the divine realm, a strong mental stand on the side of God, Love, is necessary.

A strong stand doesn't necessarily mean a loud hyped-up prayer. Audible prayers can be impressive, but we aren't here to impress, or be impressed by prayers. We *express* God, Love. As we understand what God is about, we can detect and dismiss that which does not express God, Spirit.

Informed, honest prayer is valuable. The prayer can't be pretentious. The prayer can't be bought with money. The prayer can't muddle around in superstition, idolatry, and motiveless rituals or creeds.

Godlike prayer is not defensive. If we try to defend outgrown knowledge and ideals, prayer gets twisted into useless arguments. Paul warned the Romans, "For I bear them witness that they have a zeal for God, but not according to knowledge."[5] Prayer must fit the times and needs. Sound knowledge is part and parcel to effective prayers.

Prayer becomes dangerous when it's used to gratify the senses and emotions. The regurgitation of heady words is barren. Be wise when praying or when being prayed for, because you do not want to get entangled with the deceptive prayer, disguised under good intentions. We read in Matthew, "Woe to you, scribes and Pharisees, hypocrites! You are like whitewashed tombs, which outwardly appear beautiful, but within are full of dead people's bones and all uncleanness."[6]

We can feel the aspiration, humility, gratitude, and love that our words express. We can welcome new knowledge and apply it in our prayers and lives. We don't need to waste a lot of time confessing our backward thinking, although we should never try to

---

[5] Romans 10:2
[6] Matt. 23:27

hide our mistakes. "[F]or nothing is covered that will not be revealed, or hidden that will not be known."[7]

We can examine ourselves and learn to gauge the purity of our prayer and knowledge. If we fail to examine ourselves honestly, usually our friends, or a child, can detect any self-sabotaging attitude. A true friend tells us what needs improvement and we can improve. This is not the same thing as the hyper-critical piety that gives needless criticism, doing no one any good.

You can test your prayer. Ask: Do I pray a lovely prayer and yet return to my old habits? Do I only give thanks for that which I approve of? Do I give evidence of what I am praying for? Am I loving my enemies?

It is ridiculous to congratulate yourself for loving those who love you, if you aren't blessing your enemies too.

Suffering is not God's will. We suffer when we make bad decisions, but the suffering doesn't stop us from making bad decisions. The suffering is telling us to start making better decisions.

You may hear that prayer involves taking up the cross. If you are willing to follow Christ Jesus' example, you will be expected to sacrifice, but it is a sacrifice of temporal things including hate,

---

[7] Matt. 10:26

sickness, arrogance, hypocrisy, and mindless patterns—conditions we really can live without. Prayer is the constant desire to do right, but sometimes doing right isn't pleasing in the eyes of human beings. This is the cross to bear.

As the world grows in the spiritual understanding of prayer, God will sustain us while we learn to trust the eternal and give up vain beliefs.

The world's people have many forms of prayer. Don't knock them. Experience teaches us that there is room for improvement in all forms of prayer.

We don't always receive what we ask for because we have yet fully to understand the source and means of all goodness and blessedness. Juvenile prayers were mentioned in the Bible: "When you ask, you do not receive, because you ask with wrong motives, that you may spend what you get on your pleasures."[8]

In this age, information bombards us and we are required to fine-tune our spiritual sense and knowledge. We must not be afraid to experiment and modify the knowledge circulating in earth's atmosphere.

Truth bestows no exemptions for backwardness, but wipes out all sin and sickness.

---

[8] James 4:3, NIV

Experiences vary when it comes to prayer and God. Some people hit rock bottom before acknowledging a higher power, cleaning up their act and becoming responsible and respectful. Sometimes people dabble in prayer and beg God for help. This pleading may yield an "aha" moment that reveals a spiritual identity safe with Truth, Life, and Love, but prayer feels sporadic. Then there are the prayers that try to bargain with God only to discover the deal has already been made—God gives only goodness.

To understand the healing prayer, it helps to clarify what a healing prayer is not. It is not a litany of petitions. It is not a series of repetitive affirmations. Healing prayer is not the human mind convincing itself of some grandiose idealism. It is not a deal with a humanlike God. It is not blind faith.

The healing prayer is not a faith in the human mind, in time, or in some sage or clergy who can spill out a prayer sweet as honey, but is sure to get your money.

It's fairly easy to discard the repetitious prayers that fall on deaf ears and get us nowhere. But there are other ineffective prayers, a little trickier to see and avoid. The prayer that changes one belief into another belief isn't solid. Similar to the belief that marriage will bring happiness being changed to the belief that divorce will bring happiness. Solid prayer starts with Love as the source of happiness, not with marriage or divorce.

Then there are the prayers of the do-gooders, who think they know what's best for others, but who lack a bigger view.

Whether we are praying for our self or for others, the essential foundation from which to build is spiritual understanding—an understanding of divine Spirit in control.

Healing prayer can use repetition to quiet the human ego and bring consciousness in line with a comprehending Spirit.

Prayer is a mental exercise involving spiritual understanding, not human understanding. Our prayers start with faith in God and become deep and conscientious acknowledgments of Truth. We acknowledge a knowingness that we are the image and likeness of Spirit, in full unity with Life and Love.

It is most beneficial to enter into spiritual consciousness. Our consciousness can't be riveted on the human mind, body, or condition. "We are confident, I say, and would prefer to be away from the body and at home with the Lord."[9]

God's law has given us dominion to express all the excellent, beautiful, and useful elements created by God. You can become conscious right now of the wellbeing and intelligence that is purely divine. You've been given authority—not to manage sin,

[9] II Cor. 5:8, NIV

sickness, or other people—but to experience the consciousness of intelligence, wellbeing, Truth and Love.

Although it can be useful to have other people pray for or with us, we are able to communicate directly with God without a middleperson. Turn off the television, the cellphone, the computer. Don't listen incessantly to the muscles, nerves, and brain. Enter into the heart of a healing prayer. Deny all that is unlike God and affirm wisdom, Truth, and Love. We can trust the unseen God, the Father-Mother of us all to guide us to responsible healing.

Only as we ascend above all habituated feelings and sin can we reach the heaven-born aspiration.

What is commonly referred to as the Lord's Prayer indicates the spiritual consciousness that instantaneously heals the sick. Some Bible versions include an extra line at the end, maybe added by a later copyist.

The meaning of the Lord's Prayer can be spiritually interpreted as:

Our Father in heaven,
Our Father-Mother God, all-harmonious,
Hallowed be Your name,
One sacred nature,
Your kingdom come,
Your government is come; You are ever-present,
Your will be done on earth as it is in heaven.

Enable us to know—as in heaven, so on earth—God is omnipotent, supreme.

Give us this day our daily bread.

Give us grace for today; feed the deficient intent.

And forgive us our debts, as we forgive our debtors.

And Love is reflected in love.

And lead us not into temptation, but deliver us from the evil one.

And God does not lead us into temptation, but delivers us from sin, disease, and death.

For Yours is the kingdom and the power and the glory forever.[10]

For God is infinite, all-power, all Life, Truth, Love, over all, and All.

Communion

Two forms of communion come to mind. The Christian sacrament reenacting the Lord's Last Supper where bread and wine are shared,[11] and a communion with God or the sharing of intimate thoughts on a mental or spiritual level.

Communion with God at a spiritual level can keep the tradition of sacrament from becoming either an aesthetic or anesthetic ritual.

At the Last Supper when Jesus urged his disciples to eat bread and drink wine to remember him, he

---

[10] Matt. 6:13 (NKJV)
[11] Matt. 26:26-27; Mark 14: 22-23; Luke 22:19-20; I Cor. 11:24

was pushing the concept beyond the repetitious act of eating a flake of bread and drinking wine with emotional concentration. The best way to remember Jesus is by doing what he did: commune with God, bless enemies, heal spiritually, and advocate the good news.

Communing with God, divine Mind, is oneness with God.

What does it mean to be one with the divine? If we look to Christ Jesus, we learn that divine oneness involves rules (e.g. The Golden Rule[12]) and credible inspiration. It's both an individual and collective mission. Unity with God isn't popular with the world, but it is fair to our self and merciful to others.

Oneness with the divine isn't about God coming to earth to be with human beings. Oneness with the divine isn't about Jesus dying and automatically uniting us to God. Oneness is about discovering God.

We are reconciled to the divine by attaching to the law of Spirit and detaching from the laws of matter, sin, and death. This restructuring redeems and gives us a sense of unity, rather than separation. We don't invent spirituality, but find our spirituality is inseparable from God.

---

[12] Matthew 7:12; Luke 6: 31

14

Every twinge of repentance and suffering, every effort to reform, every good thought and deed will help us to unite with the divine.

We can gain a little each day in the right direction. We can stop thinking bad thoughts about ourselves and other people, we can stop gossiping. We can engage in worthwhile activities. We can act responsibly.

Divine Truth, Life, and Love give us authority over sin, sickness, and death. We don't teach and learn a theory, doctrine, or belief system, but a life of real being. We don't practice a form of religion and worship, but practice the harmony of Life and Love.

Human beings are slow to recognize Truth. The mortal ego is reluctant or resistant to let go of its habits and imperfect perceptions. Feedback from the material world and false theologies bogs us down. They stop us from entering the door to Love.

We must advance beyond shallow thinking. Deliverance doesn't come by worshipping the personalities of spiritual masters. We can leave behind mortal impressions of fleshly existence. We can advance into immortal expressions by applying the law of God.

We must reject the attitude that our individual opinions are representative of the whole. Arrogance and fear are unprepared to bear the standard of Truth, and God will never place it in such hands.

It wasn't fair that Jesus suffered, but it's inevitable that spiritual leaders suffer some, since this is how they show us the way and power of Love and Truth. Humbly, Jesus confronted the ridicule thrown at him.

Jesus is not God. He was born of a woman. His humanness caused his struggles in Gethsemane and on Calvary, but gave us an example we could relate to. His humanity negotiated rituals, stressing that life should be used to the advantage of spiritual growth.

Jesus was deserted by all but John and the brave women who refused to turn away from spiritual goodness. The real cross which Jesus endured on the hill of misery was the world's hatred of Truth and Love.

Persecution is common in a world that generally loves a lie more than truth. Love and spiritual healing are oppressed in a world where greed and betrayal have their way. Torment occurs in a world unthankful to Spirit.

After the crucifixion, Jesus used the tomb as a refuge from the brutality of his enemies. He used it to solve the great problem of Being. His mental work opened a new era. Defended by spiritual laws, Jesus defied physical laws and mortality.

We can sanctify the supremacy of divine Mind over human mind at all times.

Church membership and taking communion won't directly unite us with God. Jesus told the church authorities and hypocritical Pharisees, "[T]he tax collectors and the prostitutes go into the kingdom of God before you."[13] The Eucharist should be a mental exercise, not only a physical ritual.

Jesus' body was the same before and after death, establishing the idea that the mortal body is not the essence of being. This image of a resurrection indicates that mortal mindsets die, while immortal mindsets live.

The Last Supper was not the last meal Jesus had with his followers. After the resurrection he ate with his disciples on the shore of the Galilean Sea.[14] Rather than focusing on the sullen supper, we can grasp the meaning of the solemn breakfast. As they ate fish, grief was transformed into repentance and the student's realized Spirit's majesty prevailed.

The spiritual growth that allowed Jesus to rise from the dead was increased even more to allow him later to ascend, prompting closure to his earthly record.

After the ascension, his students received the Holy Spirit, meaning they stopped interpreting people through human knowledge and turned their thoughts instead to divine knowledge.

---

[13] Matt. 21:31
[14] John 21

When inspired by God, Truth, and Love, we inspire others. We can serve God, rather than money. We can have pure inclinations, rather than indulge the flesh and egotism. We can drink in the spiritual evidence of health, holiness, and life, rather than absorb the material evidence of sickness, sin, and death.

Questions are posed today to people who profess to love Jesus: If that Godlike and glorified man were physically on earth today, would you reject him? Would you deny him the rights of humanity if he entertained any other lifestyle or religious practice than yours? Would you deny him the Eucharist?

The theology that thinks Jesus' crucifixion served as an immediate pardon for all sinners is undeveloped. Jesus wasn't a whipping boy. He didn't suffer so we could automatically be free to enter heaven. We use Jesus' example to learn *how* to improve, *how* to know God, *how* to stop sinning, *how* to reform. It's up to us to follow through, to go and do likewise. Showering praise on Jesus isn't enough. Superficial loyalty is flawed.

Jesus pushed the boundaries when it came to human ties. He didn't care who your parents were or what your religion was, only that you did the will of Spirit. He said, "[T]he hour is coming, and is now here, when the true worshipers will worship the

18

Father in spirit and truth, for the Father is seeking such people to worship him."[15]

Christ Jesus didn't concede to all the old traditions. He rebuked Moses' teachings of "Eye for eye,"[16] and "Whoever sheds human blood, by humans let his blood be shed."[17] Jesus showed us we can unlearn or outgrow false teachings.

We have the ability to recognize and celebrate God's omnipotence and the healing power of divine Love. The promises will be fulfilled. The time for the reappearing of the divine unity and healing is throughout all time.

Marriage

Marriage can advance spiritual goodness by serving as a legal and moral safeguard for generations to come. It gives us the opportunity to express faithfulness, virtue, mindfulness, forgiveness, and so on, while remembering that these qualities can be expressed by unmarried people also.

Marriage can improve the human species. It should not bring out the worst in partners. It can be a barrier against vice, a protection, and a discipline. Soul has infinite resources with which to bless us.

---

[15] John 4:23
[16] Exodus 21:24; Lev. 24:20; Deut. 19:21
[17] Gen. 9:6, *The Message*

Happiness is spiritual, unselfish, and must be shared. Happiness can't exist alone.

Union of the feminine and masculine qualities *represents,* not *is,* completeness. Together they should aim to reach a higher tone of courage and strength.

Abstinence from immoral or mindless sexual activity leads to an advanced state of intellectual and cultural development in human society. It offers stability and progress. Abstinence reduces unwanted pregnancies and abortions, it averts demeaning hookups and affairs. Intimacy is to be valued with integrity.

When considering a partner, look for wisdom, goodness, and truthfulness. Spiritual qualities generate a perpetual attraction between spouses.

Good looks, money, or fame only distract from harmony and fulfillment.

Before getting married, understand what it means to work as a team. Sometimes it's prudent to draw up a prenuptial agreement. A mutual understanding of one another's goals and assets should exist before, and continue after, marriage. Deception is fatal to happiness.

Ask: What do I hope for in marriage? What are my motives for marrying? What kind of goals do I pursue when with this other person? Marriage feels blessed or unblessed depending on your expectations.

Unselfish ambitions, noble life motives, and transparency can mingle together and constitute true happiness and permanence. Don't be extravagant, wasteful, or lazy. Take the time each day to be kind and keep the mutual affection clean and fresh.

Partners shouldn't demand all of one another's attention. Narrowness and jealousy swallow and bury happiness. Don't cater to a desire for incessant amusement outside the home circle. Home is the center, though not the boundary, of empathy.

Sharing the different demands in a marriage sustains an atmosphere of sweet confidence and joy. Each spouse can learn to do new chores, bringing blessings to the household.

Divorce has shown that the sacredness of marriage is losing its influence. Divorce has a way of undermining happiness, yet it can cause us to rethink marriage. From the logic of events we learn that something more than getting rid of the other partner is needed.

Divorce is a warning, not an answer. It warns us that we are too easily deceived by immaturity, selfishness, false expectations, and materialism. The powerlessness of promises becomes obvious. A reformation is in order in which the scum rises to the top to be dredged off.

When a marriage is challenged, and it will be, don't panic. Don't become self-righteous. Sorrow has its reward and never leaves us where it found us. Let inspiration and wisdom guide your decisions.

Sit down and talk with your spouse before it gets to the point where you can't talk civilly. Get a mediator if you need. Don't complain and demand; listen back and forth. Compromise, and together learn how to be efficient, economical, fair, and thoughtful when it comes to household errands, financial matters, and your sex life. Spiritual, not bossy or ungrateful, consciousness is needed. You can't fall out of Love because love is ever-present.

Trials teach us not to lean on human crutches, but on God. Remember this even when things are going well in a marriage. Use good and bad experiences to your advantage by letting new views of divine goodness and love come alive in everyday life.

Having children is a monumental responsibility. Having children doesn't prove your spouse loves you. Children will not fill a void, only God can. Being a parent means caring for, paying for, cleaning up after, setting a good example, and teaching wisely the children.

We want to diminish mistakes, give higher aims to ambition, and raise our children with attitudes and expectations worthy of perpetuity.

If parents create children who need constant attention and amusement, don't be surprised if they grow up fretful and whiny. Parents should also guard against thinking their children are more mature than they really are, as if children can make all their own decisions. Children should be allowed to remain children in innocence and open-mindedness, and become men and women through maturity, experience, and useful knowledge.

It's wise and healthy to give less intelligence to materiality and more to spirituality. Don't interfere with God's government by thrusting in your own views as if they are better than God's.

The education of children should form habits of obedience to the moral and spiritual law.

Be careful when taking on a new family dynamic. Spirituality doesn't develop when we sow seeds in the soil of material hopes as if a new family will be better. Regard wisdom, so as not to rush into a worse state of family.

Our false views of life and family produce the ills of which we complain. Life becomes convoluted when we insist our limited personal perspectives are truth. To simplify our life, we must turn instead to spiritual knowledge and put it into practice.

If you find yourself abandoned by a partner, turn to God and find people who will help you, not get even, but become independent and secure. Experience should be the school of virtue.

The epoch approaches when the truth of being will be the basis of marriage and religion. At present we progress slowly. Pride makes us believe we have it all figured out. Fear makes us reluctant to obey infinite Spirit, Love. We are slaves to mortal self-preservation, fashion, arrogance, and touchy/feely stuff. We ought to weary of the fleeting and to cherish only that which promotes our highest selfhood. Sooner or later we shall learn how Spirit, the great architect, has created us in spiritual existence.

Confidence in spiritual good must displace the mistrust that is felt when we try to trust mortals and materiality.

The divine equation includes revelation, not accumulation. It includes an imparting, not a give-and-take. Earthly challenges are overcome with the high goal in mind; coexistence with God.

We gain the sense of health, even a healthy marriage, when we lose the sense of sin and disease. To understand spiritually that there is but one creator, God, unfolds all creation and brings the sweet assurance of love and wholeness. Our real selfhood harmonizes with God and we experience unity intact.

Mind Power

Mortal existence is a fantastic mystery. Science and religion make great efforts to explain the mystery, but it is soon learned that for every answer found there are at least two more questions. Although science has moved into the cosmos of mind, scientists still do not understand how thought power works. Although religions have ventured into the realm of logic, religious practitioners and meditators have yet to grasp how spirituality systematically redeems and heals.

In a world of incomplete beliefs and theories, wisdom asks: Is the human mind or the divine Mind influencing you and others? Divine Mind dispels mystery.

The study and practice of divine Mind power is different from the conventional mind study that looks to the human mind for answers and healing. Divine Mind is power. God is power. God and God's thoughts are realities, unaffected by human minds.

Healing practices embedded in the human mind, rather than divine Mind, will always be susceptible to contradictions—good and evil, positive and negative, connection and disconnection, health and ill-health.

Mortal human mind sees what it believes as certainly as it believes what it sees. And, when the human mind is forced to see its own falsities—through experience, science, or religion—it is being prepared to loosen its grip and allow divine insight.

It is recorded that Christ Jesus read minds.[18] His mind-reading capability led to distinct spiritual healing. Mind reading is employed to expose incomplete or destructive thoughts and replace them with thoughts connected to the one Spirit, infinite Life.

Mind Reading

We can generally read an angry mind just by looking at an angry face. We read the minds of authors when we read their writings. Psychics, mediums, and healers can sometimes read human minds. However, unless the mind reading spurs spiritual growth, it is limited and appears to be supernatural, mysterious.

The spiritual ability to read thoughts and heal by the Truth-power is natural, explainable. It is achieved only as we are found, not in self-righteousness, but reflecting the divine nature.

The way by which Mind power is learned is not ecclesiastical, but humane; not physical, but metaphysical; not material, but scientific, logical, spiritual.

---

[18] Matthew 12:25; Mark 12:15; Luke 6:8, 9:47, 11:17

To read human minds unscientifically, without the input of divine Mind, is to regurgitate mortal thoughts and brain imprints. Without divine Mind, we struggle. We get distracted. We feel failure. But, don't give up because there is a Higher Power that can help, even if we "Do not know where it comes from or where it goes."[19]

Through inspiration and understanding, God reveals the spiritual knowledge that unlocks the resources of truth. Spirituality allows us to read the human situation correctly, with healing intent and power. The light of spiritual truth exposes and displaces erroneous human thoughts, and demonstrates healing.

Divine Mind power comes with spiritual courage. It requires courage to speak the truth. As you uncover mistaken thoughts, the human ego may scream to keep its convictions, but infinite thoughts prevail as the beliefs melt. In the Psalms we read, "The nations rage, the kingdoms totter; he utters his voice, the earth melts."[20]

The belief of divisible minds and the error of separation from Love can be uncovered and dissolved by the truth of one Spirit, spiritual Being. But be careful, because sometimes when you uncover error, it turns the lie on you. Don't compound the problem by insisting error is real.

---

[19] John 3:8
[20] Psalm. 46:6

Don't react as though error has an existence on par with truth. The moral demand will be met only as error is proved to be a mistake. Error is an absence of truth.

Human beings aren't spiritual. The human spirit isn't immortal. It doesn't make sense that a person living in this world has a spirit constrained by a physical body, yet after death will live in another world as the spirit. Does it carry all the emotional baggage and human knowledge from this world? If this were so, and if the spirit had the option to return to this world, why would we want to communicate with a spirit that hasn't really advanced past fluxing limited perceptions?

Why get answers from someone who thinks death has had, or will have, an impact on Spirit, Life? Why believe we live in, or die out of, the body? Why believe there is a limbo land between the living and the dead? Why assume we are hastening to death, yet communing with life?

There is one Spirit, and it is communicating useful knowledge to us. Spirit isn't divided into spirits and life isn't dealt out with beginnings and endings. God is our Life.

There is one spiritual existence, not many levels of existence. If human mind were permeated by Spirit, its manifestation would disappear to physical sense and appear deathless. But probably death will occur on the next plane of existence as on this, until the spiritual understanding of Life is reached. Then, and not until then, will it be demonstrated that, "Over such the second death has no power."[21]

Useful mind-reading starts and ends with the one Spirit, eternal Life.

The truth of spiritual existence motivates a healing mind practice. Spiritual existence is sinless joy, complete harmony, and divine nature. Our spirituality possesses ongoing beauty, goodness, and holy purpose without a single bodily pleasure or pain.

Thought Control

The power of thought continues to be a hot topic. The fields of psychology, psychiatry, counseling, and hypnotism have been opened up and are being cultivated by a significant portion of the population. Brains are probed and studied extensively. The potential of mind over matter draws attention from all corners of the world.

Mind forces exist. Thoughts can be very powerful. In the 20th century, Carl Jung[22] classified three human psychic levels: (1) consciousness, (2) the personal unconscious, and (3) the collective unconscious.

---

[21] Revelation 20:6
[22] Jung, Carl Gustav (1875-1961) Swiss psychiatrist and founder of the school of analytical psychology.

Mental health is important, but when looked for in the human mind, health feels precarious, almost imaginary. We read about philosophical and psychological loops creating paranoia, making us scrutinize every single thought floating in the mental milieu. We read about theories based on studies showing that societal issues, from workplace rudeness to weight gain, are contagious.[23] Yet, why don't we grasp why the personal or collective unconscious can make us do things we wouldn't normally do?

We read about cutting-edge neurotechnology used to govern prosthetic limbs geared to respond to electrical commands from the brain. But are these electrical commands reliable? Do they vary from one brain to another? Do they point to many minds, some of which may be nefarious?

Even though the study of thought power and technology have become sophisticated, we still don't understand how to control our minds and bodies, whether or not we have real or artificial parts.

When studying mind, we must learn the difference between human thoughts and divine thoughts. We must guard our self against any situation where

---

[23] Catching Rudeness Is Like Catching a Cold: The Contagion Effects of Low-Intensity Negative Behaviors. http://psycnet.apa.org accessed 9/2015; New evidence for link between teens' social network, weight gain http://www.loyolamedicine.org accessed 9/2015

human thoughts control our own, whether it's through crowd thinking, brainwashing, peer pressure, superstition, hypnotism, mesmerism, magic, necromancy, or technology, all based in the theory that mind is in matter.

The thoughts of human beings have nothing to do with divine Mind. Although some human thoughts are better than others, to give them power is— unconsciously and automatically—to give power to the evil thoughts also held in human minds. This despotism is but a phase of nothingness and is removed by spirituality.

Human knowledge is defined as that which comes from the belief that Mind is dividable or isolatable. The human mind experiences its own limited knowledge. Mind study becomes risky and suffering is prolonged when we wrongly give separate human minds power to control life or the world. God is power.

God is Life, God is substance. God is Mind. God is good. Divine knowledge is identified as that which comes from the one Mind. It leads to goodness, unselfishness, forgiveness, humility, bravery. Divine knowledge follows the law of progress.

We must spiritually think for ourselves and image forth divine knowledge; otherwise, indifferent, self-destructive, and depressed behavior is believed to be our own thinking and it will be exhibited. We also need to encourage in others their right and responsibility to know and act on divine thoughts.

Don't build up evil.

Divine knowledge exists, is in force, and has ultimate power. Divine thoughts are intelligent, fruitful, unified; they belong to us. As we escape from the claims of human mind, the whole human family is blessed and virtue is promoted in the community. But we can be duped again by the ignorant or malicious teachings that result in physical limitations or moral idiocy.

The mild forms of mortal thought-control disappear and more aggressive features come to the fore. Threatening, terrorizing, and bigoted thoughts, created and harbored in human minds, are weaving webs of more complicated and subtle crimes, providing a steady stream of fodder for human mind study.

To stay on guard against the mortal claims, we must acknowledge, study, and demonstrate thoughts of the one good Spirit. Spirituality must become the basis of our thought process.

Spiritual growth counters the temptations to either languish in states of indolence and apathy, or jump into extremist actions. We can discover that the human mind, even bulked together with many minds, is powerless before divine Mind.

The mental qualities of dishonesty, lethargy, revenge, malice, and arrogance will not heal the sick. If they appear to, it is temporary and leaves the case worse than before.

In divine Mind there is no human mortal mindedness, there is no transference of mortal memes and false teachings.

We must consider the motives behind mind study. What is motivating power? Is it money or modesty? Is it jealousy or justice? Is it lust or love? Is it fear or moral courage? Is it personal power or healing?

Life and being are of God, the source of true thoughts, passing from God to us. Evil has no reality in divine Mind.

The development of our mental powers must be done with God, Love. God has given us the rights of self-control, logic, and conscience. We are properly self-governed when guided and compelled by Truth and Love.

Science, Theology, and Medicine

The law of Life, Truth, and Love inspires the disciplines of science, theology, and medicine with a more divine nature and essence. The law is Spirit.

Spirit and existence is natural, but not physical or measurable. Life is alive, but not biological. Reality is normal, but not supernatural or mysterious. Healing through the power of Spirit is possible and has occurred for millenniums.

We can spiritually discern and live by divine laws. We can outgrow false beliefs that work against progress. We can break barriers in ways that benefit humanity through an understanding of Spirit. The spiritual method of healing is lost sight of now and then, but its truth remains to be discerned and experienced.

We can understand and practice the one Spirit or divine Mind that governs the entire creation by using the power of Truth to extinguish erroneous concepts. We can perceive that all cause and effect belong to Spirit.

When people try to attribute cause and effect to matter or human energy, they can't find a first physical cause; it's the chicken and egg quandary, unanswered. It's no wonder the human race yearns for Spirit and spirituality.

The following view of reality is proposed:

- There is more to reality than the human evidence;
- Divine Mind and its reality can be experienced as human mind gives way to divine laws;
- All real being is in God, the divine Mind;
- Matter and human energy don't possess sensation or life;
- Sin, sickness, disease, and death are subjective states of human mind;
- Spirit is Life.

People glimpse divine healing, but human opinions, arrogance, ignorance, and greed often interfere. An understanding of divine healing is also impeded by the inadequacy of human languages from which to articulate metaphysical concepts. The vital part, the mind, heart, and soul of the divine workings, is not words, but Love. Without love, words are empty.

To glimpse divine metaphysics, try thinking about this: There is no pain in Truth, and no truth in pain; there is no nerve in Mind, and no mind in nerve; there is no illusion in Mind, and no mind in illusion; there is no good in bad, and no bad in good; there is no intelligence in matter, and no matter in intelligence; there is nothing impermanent in the permanent, and nothing permanent in the impermanent; there is no flesh in Spirit, and no Spirit in flesh.

God is Mind. God is substance. God is energy. If substance and energy is Mind, they are not the changing substance and energy we call matter or quantum energy. The human mind has no power over divine Mind.

The term *human mind* is really a misnomer. The mortal human mind always dies. Was it ever a mind, knowing life? The human mind and its images of flesh and body is temporary and opposes eternal Mind.

The human mind is limited, undeveloped, immature, and projects itself through what we call matter or human energy. Another way to view the human mind is in three degrees:

First degree: Depravity. The depraved state is attached to physical or materialist energy. It includes evil beliefs, addictions and appetites, fear, corrupt willfulness, hatred, envy, arrogance, deceit, sickness, disease, death, self-righteousness.

Second degree: Improvement. Depraved thinking and thoughts are being replaced with moral thoughts and behaviors that express humanity, honesty, empathy, hope, faith, humility, and moderation.

Third degree: Understanding. This state is radiant with wisdom, purity, spiritual comprehension and power, love, health, and holiness.

In the third degree, human logic yields to revelation and enlightened logic. The image and likeness of God appears and human mind and its images disappear. Divinity is witnessed as all-inclusive and the spiritual universe is experienced as intact.

To neglect infinite Spirit is to start insisting matter and human energy is the reality and is self-evolved and self-governing, yet there is no beginning or end. If you believe in a humanlike God, it may be assumed that matter was created by Spirit. These insistences and assumptions suck us into a vicious vortex of contradictions, even making God responsible for all disasters.

Mysteries disappear through discovery and revelation. Scientists, meteorologists, physicians, and computer programmers remove mystery from weather, the body, or electronics. Old-time restraints become extinct when science modifies theories such as when absolutes were replaced with the theory of relativity. Time and space have wrinkled as we fly around the earth in jets. Matter particles are dodged or switched out, no longer seen as solid mass. We can likewise remove mystery from the study of nature and life through spiritual knowledge and divine consciousness.

Technology shows that connectivity exists, but material connectivity is fragile and can break-up.

Connectivity exists in divine Mind. In Mind-science, we discover that matter and its human mind is only an echo, with no real substance or power to break, sicken, or derail Spirit and our spiritualty.

We overcome limitations by reflecting God's government and being self-governed.

Health is not a condition of physical atoms but of infinite Mind. Freedom is not a circumstance of temporal life but of eternal Life. Spirituality is not a power of measured force but of immeasurable force.

While working out the laws of Mind, things are resolved into thoughts. The objects of physical sense are replaced with spiritual ideas. Human perceptions fade as we find divine perceptions clear and thriving. The key is spiritual discovery.

Theology

Divine theology and popular theology differ. Anything and everything entitled to a classification as divine must be comprised of knowledge or a logical understanding of God, illimitable Mind, whereas popular theology is comprised in knowledge of mortal existence.

Unfortunately, we are ingrained in false beliefs that war against spiritual facts. The false must be denied and cast out to make place for truth. Jesus' love for little children reminds us of the need to be receptive to new ideas.[24] Don't wait for a catastrophe to get the attention of your spiritual consciousness. Right now, you can shake off your faith in the false and your faith in God can blossom.

When first discovering Spirit and divine logic, the sinner stiffens when realizing that sin must be destroyed. The petty intellect shudders to think it must stop trying to preserve its own personal theological knowledge. The impious attitude has a difficult time restraining itself from exploiting spirituality. The human ego will rebel or be reluctant to improve, when discovering Spirit.

The spiritual idea and the people who present it should not be ignored in order to retain materialistic beliefs about God.

Doubt evil. Forsake evil. Don't be startled at the brisk claims of evil. Evil is the belief that good is absent. Instead, think it natural to love good. Cultivate the reality of health and spiritual power.

God is not the author of disease, trauma, melodrama, abuse, or demise—and those evils, if you will, have no law to support them. What produces laws? Do atoms or human minds produce laws? If they do, they can be undone by divine Mind.

---

[24] Matt. 19:13-14; Mark 10:13-14; Luke 18:15-16

The laws of divine Mind are good. God is good, all-power.

Good is uncomplicated. Good is not miraculous to itself. Spiritual good, properly understood, is practical. People have found that the application of divine logic improves their level of perseverance and mental powers. Spiritual understanding parallels deeper insight and people are better able to understand one another.

The law of God improves and expands our character and alertness. We discover that it increases stamina, resiliency, and the ability to multitask. Immortal knowledge develops our dormant potential.

Divine knowledge is accessible, even if the churches seem not ready to approach it. Scripture says, "He came to that which was his own, but his own did not receive him."[25] Don't discount the spiritual idea in order to preserve beloved rituals and past successes. And don't abuse a truth to infuriate another person.

Throughout history and in a multitude of cultures we find it is Mind that saves. Only when we depart from the true idea, does demoralization seep in and distract us away from divine Mind.

Miracles can happen anywhere and at any time, because Mind is ever-present. Miracles are natural.

---

[25] John 1:11, NIV

Spirit is fully capable of making the body harmonious.

Recognize no life, mind, intelligence, nor substance outside of God, divine Mind. This means we can't argue for static traditions, dogmas, or a supernatural God, all of which can lead to damaging authoritative positions.

There is divine authority for believing in the superiority of spiritual power over material resistance. The same power that heals sin also heals sickness.

Christian theology is more than a profession of a deep abiding love for Christ Jesus and God. To adhere to Jesus' divine theology is to let go of our cherished attachments to human personality and grasp Christ as Truth.

Tyranny and arrogance need constantly to be cleaned out of church temples and codes. The vanity of superficial worship needs to be purged. It is more important to welcome the stranger at the church door than to build a fabulous edifice.

Spirituality isn't in limited supply. It isn't controlled by a person or organization. The spiritual idea and its healing power can't be monopolized. The widespread belief that only specific people are entitled to spiritual authority implodes in light of the

Biblical stand that all believers "will be called priests of the Lord."[26]

We can adopt a spiritual theology. We can heal divinely. We can give the spiritual equation justice and fair representation in the media. We can know and practice divine theology.

Medicine

The medicine of divine Mind *is* divine Mind. The medicine involves metaphysical treatment, working out the divine equation in which the human mind yields to divine Mind and relies on God for healing. The nature and the character of Mind is the remedy for that which works against life, truth, and love. They are one and the same.

The medicine of divine Mind is unlike the invented medicines of human minds.

Due to the dualistic or relativistic natures of human minds and medicines, humanity is driven to choose between remedies—usually choosing the lesser remedy to relieve the greater problem. But this creates more problems and pill is added to pill and surgery to surgery. Health becomes a struggle. The struggle, however is not between human minds. The struggle is between human minds and immortal Mind.

---

[26] Ex. 19:6; Isa. 61:6; Rev. 1:6

Our spiritual awareness relieves the human mind from falling back on itself. It allows a reliance on the available superiority of divine Mind.

Instead of looking to human persons and material units for guidance and deliverance, we can look to divine Principle. It doesn't matter what temporary method you adopt, whether faith in drugs, trust in surgery, or a reliance on some other cure, the victory is reached only when human belief yields to immortal Mind.

The will of Truth must supersede human willpower. True progress in medicine isn't achieved by human willpower or more money.

Willing the sick to recover is not the metaphysical practice of the divine healing. Human willpower can lead to ignorance, obsession, or risky crazes, therefore it must be kept secondary to the divine will of Truth.

To mix material and spiritual treatments is to dilute the treatment. Why is it difficult for healers to rely only on divine Mind for healing? Because our faith in drugs, surgery, or mysticism is stronger than our faith in God.

Instant gratification, faith in matter, and radicalism have become obstacles to divine healing. Symptoms, rather than the cause, are treated and conventional medicine has a difficult time maintaining success. Supposedly cured diseases are replaced by more complex diseases. Drugs are dicey and can affect people differently, oftentimes causing terrible side effects, or they become useless. Surgeries also are chancy and sometimes set the stage for fatal infections.

We know the human mind can affect the body so why don't we push the question and discover how divine Mind controls the mind and body? We don't because spiritual knowledge *will* go against what is commonly taught in anatomy, biology, theology, sociology, and genetics. But, without becoming offended or defensive, we can use divine logic and revelation to get to know the healing power of Truth and wisdom.

The medicine of Truth isn't eccentric or exclusive. Its mission isn't to maintain mortal bodies or make human minds powerful, but is to replace all that opposes God, Life, Truth, Love. Truth has a healing effect, even when not fully understood.

The doctrine of the superiority of matter and human mind can continue to fade. Placebos teach us that beliefs or expectations can affect the body. Homeopathic, holistic, and yoga practices have decreased reliance on medicinal drugging.

Divine metaphysics is the next stately step. Its principle includes a Truth that neutralizes and destroys mistaken theories. Problems are addressed logically, from the premise of divine Spirit. Fear is recognized as a culprit that needs to be restrained and removed.

In divine metaphysics, or Christian Science as defined by Mary Baker Eddy in the 19th century, mental conditions are taken into account. The metaphysician agrees with health and challenges disease mentally. This spiritual and profound pathology embraces the preventative and curative arts.

Great respect is due to the motives and philanthropy of thoughtful theologians, physicians, and researchers. With due appreciation to professionals and experts, here are a few statements worth thinking about:

"The materials we need to reach a new level of discourse are in our grasp; we have only to abandon outmoded approaches/disciplines to achieve an enlightening beginning for a new science." From *The Anthropology of Medicine: From Culture to Method,* Third Edition.[27]

"The Starting Point of Biblical Theology: We have already observed that every scholarly endeavor

---

[27] *The Anthropology of Medicine: From Culture to Method,* Third Edition. Edited by Lola Romanucci-Ross, Daniel E. Moerman, Laurence R. Tancredi. Copyright © 1997 by Lola Romanucci-Ross, Daniel E. Moerman, and Laurence R. Tancredi. Reproduced with permission of Greenwood Publishing Group, Inc., Westport, CT.

inevitably is based upon presuppositions."[28]
HarperCollins Bible Dictionary.

"We physicians often pay lip service to the importance of the mind in health and illness, yet in practice we equate it with the brain. This is obvious in our reliance on drugs when mental problems arise…. A refreshing contrast is alternative or complementary medicine, which has emerged as a major social force shaping medical care in the United States." From *Reinventing Medicine: Beyond Mind/Body to a New Era of Healing.*[29]

"We know from history that much of what doctors do at any particular time is ineffective or even dangerous when viewed in retrospect. Years ago a famous professor warned his graduating medical students that half of what he'd taught them was wrong, but the trouble was he didn't know which half. Medical practice has evolved significantly since then, but the principle still applies: we don't know which of the well-intentioned therapies of the present will end up looking like the leeches and bloodletting of ancient time or like the thalidomide, Dalkon shields, and routine tonsillectomies of a more recent era gone by. Accordingly, the pronouncements of doctors should be

---

[28] *HarperCollins Bible Dictionary.* Paul J. Achtemeier, General Editor, With the Society of Biblical Literature (HarperCollins Publishers, New York: 1996)

[29] *Reinventing Medicine: Beyond Mind/Body To a New Era of Healing,* by Larry Dossey, M.D. (HarperCollins, NY:1999)

viewed with healthy skepticism."[30] Timothy B. McCall, M.D. a practicing physician in Boston.

"We physicians do not fully understand the relationship between mind, body, and that intangible element known as spirit.... Medical educators have often taught that religion is an irrelevant or even detrimental factor in physical and emotional well-being. But a growing body of research has established that religious people, both young and old, often enjoy the psychological and physical benefits of a positive emotional outlook."[31] Harold G. Koenig, M D., Director of Duke University's Center for the Study of Religion/Spirituality and Health.

A sampling of other recommended reading: *Complications: A Surgeon's Notes on an Imperfect Science,* by Atul Gawande; *A History of God: The 4,000-Year Quest of Judaism, Christianity and Islam*, by Karen Armstrong; *Second Opinions: Stories of Intuition and Choice in the Changing World of Medicine*, by Jerome Groopman; *The Future of Faith*, by Harvey Cox.

It is right to say that the educated class of scientists and medical doctors are great people. They are more scientific than are false claimants to the divine healing method. There is much that yet remains to be said and done before all humankind is saved and before all the mental microbes of sin and disease

---

[30] McCall, Timothy B., *Examining Your Doctor: A Patient's Guide to Avoiding Harmful Medical Care.* New York: Carol Publishing, 1995
[31] Koenig, Harold G. *The Healing Power of Faith: Science Explores Medicine's Last Great Frontier.* New York: Simon and Shuster, 1999.

thought-germs are exterminated. Mistakes will be made, but it is fair to say that mistakes can't wholly obscure the divine Mind and its continuing revelation of Truth as the best medicine.

Physiology and Genetics

Physiology and genetics may have apparent powers, but they can't successfully assume the place and power of the divine source of all health and enlightenment. Drugs, DNA, and human minds can't improve God's work.

We want to keep our immortal consciousness open to spiritual existence and to our God-given powers.

From the self-conflicted human mind comes an inharmonious body. Diseases multiple even when we try to follow a physical routine as if what we eat, how much we sleep, and how much we exercise will remedy our aches and pains.

Brain, heart, blood, DNA, bone structure, etc. are not our identity. If they were, we'd lose part of our identity when we donate blood. Physiology and genetics don't define us and they can't determine our future.

Intellect, health, strength, and beauty are tied to spiritual understanding, not to material knowledge gained from the study of physiology and genetics. Material knowledge mutates, changes. Why believe intellect, health, strength, and beauty are at the mercy of non-intelligent DNA or material atoms?

Why not enlist your belief on the side of spirituality and understand immutable divine Mind? All cause and effect belong to divine Mind. Spiritual cause is the one question that gets us on the right track. Spiritual cause relates to human progress. We can approach this subject and explore the supremacy of Spirit.

As we evolve in our knowledge of physiology and genetics, we can mentally discern cause, rather than focus on effect. Academics of the right sort are requisite. Whatever galvanizes an idea governed by God is food for thought. Observation, invention, study, and original thoughts are expansive and should advance consciousness into the immortal.

If our consciousness gets stuck in the downward spiral of believing symptoms are causes—or of depending on matter, dogma, or the human mind for treatment—we can reverse our direction by obeying spiritual law. "Where your treasure is, there your heart will be also."[32] With the aid of divine inspiration and spiritual logic, our consciousness can advance out of weariness and disease, out of that which hides the power of Spirit.

The legitimate and only possible action of divine Mind is the production of harmony.

Why do drugs alleviate human ailments? Because we believe drugs can heal. But that belief is unreliable. It can easily backfire. The drug can lose its power to heal, or no longer be available, or we can become addicted to the drug.

---

[32] Matt. 6:21; Luke 12:34

The human thought must free itself from self-imposed materiality and the apprehension of mortal life. Steer away from asking the brain, heart, or lungs, "How will my day go?" Ask divine Mind.

To speculate whether we originated from "the dust of the ground,"[33] an egg, or monkeys, only gives us debatable arguments. None of those elements form a link to Spirit.

Hormones, neurons, or RNA manifests limited mentality. Arguing for limited thinking reduces truth to the level of error. Spirit never passes through insensible matter. Soul never is or was stuck in a physical body.

Disease is a latent belief in human mind, it is mental. It is a result of education and carries its ill-effects as far as human mind plots out. It is the human mind that produces disorder and hysteria. It is the human mind—not the material body—that feels, suffers, and enjoys.

Human mind and body are one and the same, like sand and rock, like water and ice. A material body is an embodied concept within the human mind. We must understand that the cause of disease obtains in the human mind, and the cure comes from the immortal divine Mind.

Human minds don't comprehend mortal existence and they can barely grasp the intuition that there is

---

[33] Genesis 2:7

something greater than themselves. We need to comprehend the greater, and learn properly how to rely on spiritual intuition and consciousness in healing work.

Overcome beliefs instead of restrict yourself to them. We can uproot disease and throw it out of the mind. We can comprehend that disease is not a fixed fact. We can feel the influence of divine Love casting out fear. Spiritual consciousness masters fear instead of avoids or cultivates it. The more that is said about moral and spiritual law, the better will be the quality of life and the further mortals will be removed from mental illness or disease.

Spiritual consciousness guides us to locate and employ physicians who see us as more than just a physical body. Honest conversations with practitioners are appropriate.

We don't need to be negatively affected by advertisements paid for by pharmaceutical companies. It's beneficial not to give time and attention to selfishness, coddling, or fear-based guessing about our minds and bodies. It's beneficial not to discuss our maladies with others as if it's a competition to see who is worse off.

The latest food fad is not a health law. Heredity is not a law. Heredity is a breakable string of past and present mortal thoughts.

It's beneficial not to pursue exaggerated or harmful ideologies. What are you watching day and night? We don't need to submit to intellect-insulting entertainment that caters to dark amusement rather than enlightened improvement. What are you enabling? We can stay safe from the age-old habit of thinking we need to get the latest disease, or worse, get a new bizarre sickness.

No law exists to support mortality and its sin, sickness, and destruction. Sin makes its own hell and goodness its own heaven. If you are comfortable in the mortal life dream, some type of suffering can poke you to waken.

Every human being must learn that evil has neither power nor reality in Spirit. Evil is a denial of truth, as if Truth could be absent, but it can't. There is no absence of God, omnipotent and omnipresent good.

Evil is self-assertive, but its only power is to destroy itself. Evil is not immortal; if it was, goodness would be a myth. Every attempt of evil to destroy good is a failure and only aids in punishing the evildoer. Do not concede reality to disorder while dealing with it realistically.

Drugs are powered by the thoughts behind them. The more believers that believe the drug has power, the more powerful the drug. But bear in mind, those believers also know the drug is toxic, therefore if a person overdoses or takes a poisonous drug by accident, death could result. The result is controlled by the majority of opinions, however, divine Mind, understood, can reverse the opinions.

The sins of other people should not make good people suffer.

A strong, well-rounded intellect coincides with spiritual law. In and of themselves, physiology and genetics are helpless. Mind is not helpless. Intelligence is not mute before non-intelligence. Our spirituality reflects divine intelligence.

Footsteps of Truth

What is Truth? The efforts of any *ology* to answer this question are vain.

Understanding comes through spiritual logic and revelation. Following the signposts of divine law, we comprehend the Truth that is changing the world for the better. In this path we find progress attended by life and peace.

We do not need to learn our life lessons the hard way. We can stop stumbling around in drunkenness. We can stop being consumed by disease. We can stop being shocked at the evil in the world and gain an understanding that leads to productive improvement.

This metaphysical system of healing through truth relinquishes the errors of self-serving obsessions, misleading appetites, hatred, fear, lust, superstition, etc. The progression makes a new creation.[34] The way to uncover and abandon error is to saturate the mind with floodtides of Truth and Love.

The opposite of Truth is error; however, knowledge of error and its operations must precede the understanding of the Truth that destroys error. Step by step we learn error is that which opposes divine Spirit and our spirituality.

---

[34] II Cor. 5:17

As we discover there is one Mind, the divine law of loving our neighbor as ourselves is unfolded. We experience a relationship with all the attributes of Truth and Love, including wisdom. We become conscious of the existence of Spirit as the source of supply.

If Spirit created sickness and disorder, then it would be wrong or impossible for human beings to try and remove them. Sickness and death are awful deceptions of existence, not put forth by Truth.

The brain, nerves, hormones, and stomach can't talk on their own. They act because of mind. Sensations of the body are sensations of the human mind. Through Truth you discover your ability to embrace your body and outline it with thoughts of health.

Let us prepare for the supremacy of Spirit—the government and law of universal harmony, which cannot be lost or remain forever unseen.

All the faculties of Mind are intact. No matter where we are, we can use our spiritual senses to commune with God and be governed by Love.

To be controlled by divine Mind is not to be controlled by hypnotism, human cultures, theories, crime, drugs, or fantasies. We learn to utilize spiritual sense—the constant conscious capacity to understand the all-acting infinite Spirit.

The cruel narcissistic tendencies inherent in human mind are always germinating new forms of tyranny and must be rooted out through the action of the divine Mind. To rid the world of terrorists is difficult, but to destroy mental terrorism is even more difficult.

Healing systems must have spirituality in order to be useful. Medicines and religions dictated by money, status-quo, inequality, rituals, and regulations only imitate the old-time opposition that upset Jesus two thousand years ago. "So, he made a whip out of cords, and drove all from the temple courts, both sheep and cattle; he scattered the coin of the money changers and overturned their tables."[35]

Let Truth regenerate the fleshly mind and feed thought with the bread of Life. Food should not be given more power than God. The only diet that works is the diet that follows a mental plan involving honesty, wisdom, hard work, and balance. "This I say then, Walk in the Spirit, and ye shall not fulfill the lust of the flesh."[36]

It is impossible to form our concepts of Truth from what is seen between the cradle and the grave. We don't pass from mortality to immortality, or from evil to good. Evil dies and good continues its immortal expression. The infinite never began and will never end.

---

[35] John 2:15, NIV
[36] Galatians 5:16, KJV

We marvel at the people who live to be old and yet stay healthy and useful. They become objects of intrigue. Science may attribute the longevity to genes and environment, but these theories are never found to be consistent. A better theory is attached to attitude.

Why not have the attitude that soaks up the radiance of Soul and appreciates each year's unfolding of wisdom, aplomb, and holiness? Why not shape our views of existence into loveliness, newness, and continuity, rather than into doom and gloom?

Measuring and limiting all that is beautiful and good is unproductive. Beauty and truth are eternal, but the beauty of physical things passes away. Don't get hung up on superficial attractiveness, dictated by the media or the latest fashion. Beauty is an element of life, forever in Mind and fully expressed through us. Mind feeds the body with freshness and fairness, supplying it with comforting images of thought.

The recipe for beauty is to have less illusion and more Soul. Body piercings, Botox, and breast augmentation are poor substitutes for true beauty.

Clothe yourself with Truth as opposed to wrapping yourself up in speculations or superstitions. Truth has no consciousness of error. Love has no sense of hate. Life has no partnership with death. Truth, Life, and Love are a law of annihilation to everything unlike themselves.

The advancement of Truth has nothing to do with popularity. The object is to work in the interest of humanity, not work in private interests or sect. No matter what field you work in, Truth should stimulate labor and progress.

Wealth, fame, and social organizations have no pull with God. We get better views of humanity when we level wealth with sincerity, break up cliques and cults, and let worth be judged according to wisdom. Success in error is defeat in Truth, but the wicked person is not the ruler of the upright. Our motto is, "Let the wicked forsake their ways and the unrighteous their thoughts."[37]

Here are a few unrighteous or ineffective mental practices:

- Unwillingness to welcome new ideas;
- Reluctance to consider the deception of material laws and human energy;
- Repeating thought patterns as if they are law;
- Believing sin is unfixable.

To fear sin is to misunderstand the power of Love and your relationship to God. Holding yourself superior to sin, because God made you superior to it, is true wisdom. It is equally wise to hold yourself

---

[37] Isaiah 55:7, NIV

superior to sickness and disorder in accordance with the Holy Spirit.

When you understand God, you will no longer fear sin and sickness because they are no part of spiritual revelation and existence.

The pursuit of understanding God requires proper gear and backup. Put up a firewall of love against sick thoughts, lusts, and horrible intents. Regularly clean the mind of any sin and sickness. Control evil thoughts in the first instance or they will control you in the second. Radiate uprightness and honesty. Be practical and reasonable, not a showoff.

Be aware of and don't follow the mental mal-practitioner who doesn't obey Truth, but twists thoughts to suit their own narrow agenda and creed. You'd rather ask for help from a doctor who has the flu than ask for help from a mental mal-practitioner, even if they claim to be a spiritual Shaman, Psychic, Shaykh, Caliph, Christian Science practitioner, etc.

Parents are the strongest educators for their children. The thoughts of the parents form the embryo of another mortal mind. It is better to form the embryo consciously after the model of divine Mind rather than form it unconsciously after a human model. After birth, continue to form children with divine influences, teaching them self-government, happiness, receptivity, and the Truth-cure.

We move toward good or evil as time passes. Past failures will be repeated until we destroy spiritual idleness, self-gratification, shameless competitiveness, blaming others, envy, hypocrisy, hate, revenge, and materialism.

Let's compare the testimony of human mind against the testimony of Spirit:

> Human mind lifts its voice with the arrogance of reality and says: I can steal, cheat, lie, commit adultery, murder, retaliate and yet avoid detection by flattering words. I am dishonest, yet no one knows it. My inclinations and sentiments can be irrational, deceitful, and fraudulent. My purpose is to make this short span of life one big fling. The world is my domain. I'm ecstatic to think of the power of sin, albeit I admit, that an accident, an epiphany, or the law of God can at any moment annihilate my peace. My efforts to express life are fatal. I'm like bursting lava—I blow up only to fall to despair in a consuming fire.

> Divine Spirit says: I am Spirit. Man and woman, whose perceptions are spiritual, are my likeness. You reflect the infinite understanding, for I am infinity. What belongs to me belongs to you—the beauty of holiness, the completion of being, and imperishable glory. I am immortal Truth; therefore, you are immortal and truthful. I

include and impart all bliss, for I am Love. I give life, without beginning and without end, for I am Life. I am the substance of all because "I AM WHO I AM."[38]

Incomplete human beings get flustered when following Truth, but don't give up. Be practical when abandoning the material for the spiritual. Eat healthy food, exercise wisely, work with integrity, use common sense, and be law abiding while you discover your spirituality.

The human footsteps are indispensable. Truth seekers are consistent who, watching and praying, can "Run and not be weary...walk and not be faint."[39] We can gain spirituality rapidly and hold our position, or we can attain slowly and yield not to discouragement. God requires our due diligence. The battle between Spirit and flesh is fought and the spiritual facts of existence are reached step by step before the victory is won.

---

[38] Exodus 3:14
[39] Isaiah 40:31

Creation

Creation is more than what the eye sees and the human mind knows. As we outgrow our limited mentalities and knowledge, thought expands into expression. "Let there be light,"[40] is the perpetual demand of Love, changing chaos into order and revealing Truth's universe.

As thought progresses from the material to the spiritual, from the scholastic to the inspirational, from the mortal to the immortal, it finds Mind, not matter. It finds Love.

Time-based concepts do not bring about an understanding of God. It's better to ask and explore: What is infinite Mind or divine Love?

Infinite Mind is the creator and creation is the infinite image or idea emanating from this Mind. Spirit is the only substance. Spirit, Soul, is never controlled by the body or human mind.

We are more than minds trapped in physical forms. We reflect infinity. We express what we know about God, Truth. Our capabilities increase as our conception of the divine increases. We can conceive of our nature as never born and never dying.

It is with spiritual sense that we discern the heart of infinity. Immortal ideas are ever-present, although

---

[40] Gen. 1:3

sometimes clouded by mortal thoughts and illusions.

Humans must improve their ideals in order to improve their models. Sick thoughts evolve sick bodies. Selfishness evolves not only carnal pains, but also the carnal pleasures that bring disappointment.

When we look to the flesh for life, we find death. When we look to matter for comfort, we find discomfort. When we look to the physical earth for truth, we find impermanence and confusion. Now, turn away from flesh and earth and look toward Truth and Love, the origin of all happiness, harmony, and immortality.

Think about it: we can detach from the body to a degree, unconsciously, when we become so absorbed in a movie or activity that we forget our body. So, detach instead from the body—as a form of human belief—and learn the meaning of God and creation.

Spiritual consciousness requires a mental effort. We start with thought and work patiently to conquer all that is unlike God. We have to begin at the highest standpoint possible. Start with mind instead of brain. Start with humanity instead of egotism. Start with spiritual history rather than mortal history. Start with God instead of many creators.

There is only one creator, one Being. Whatever seems to be a new creation is but the discovery of some previously unknown idea of Truth, or a break-off from an old mortal thought.

The fleeting concepts of the human mind have their day before the permanent facts of Spirit appears. Immature mortal thoughts will grow out of themselves and finally give place to the glorious ideas of divine Mind.

Look where you walk and act as though you possess the power given to you by God.

Every stumble, every loss, every disappointment, every tinge of pain can be used to break through the barriers of the problem and discover what belongs to wisdom and Love. Each time we gain more correct views of God, the invisible becomes visible. Life expands into self-completeness and we find all in God.

If you are one of those people who can't live without friends, don't be surprised when those friends stop giving you sympathy. Friends will betray and enemies will slander. When you find you are feeling alone, use the occasion as a chance to accept what best promotes your own spiritual growth and advancement in Love.

"Blessed is the man who remains steadfast under trial, for when he has stood the test he will receive the crown of life, which God has promised to those who love him."[41] Love never leaves you. We don't cross some line to reach Love. We coexist with Love.

Spirit and its formations are the only realties of being.

[41] James 1:12

Being

Thought expands toward real Being as it yields to the idea that all cause and effect belong to Mind, rather than to matter. It's a slow process and can be tumultuous. Physical theories challenge metaphysics to meet in final combat. In this revolutionary period, like the shepherd boy[42] with his sling and stones, metaphysics goes forth to battle with the Goliaths of materialism and physics. Being is divine Spirit, Mind, and Mind's ideas.

Semi-metaphysical systems afford no substantial aid. We learn to separate the material and spiritual in order to discover effective metaphysics and the reality of divine Being.

The literal interpretation of Scripture has made God humanlike. The spiritual interpretation makes heaven and earth and their inhabitants Godlike. The first is error, the latter is truth.

The divine interpretation of God's law reveals understanding and harmony.

Spiritual interpretation rests on one basis, the divine Mind. The ideas of Mind are real and tangible to spiritual consciousness. Mind's ideas have the advantage of being real and good, whereas objects and thoughts of physical sense are contradictory and not absolute. Moreover, physical senses have no

---

[42] I Samuel 17

direct link to Spirit. Material, measurable units don't enter into metaphysical premises or conclusions.

Secular interpretations of Being try to divide intelligence into human minds, whereas divine Mind, our Mind, is indivisible. These old beliefs of divisibility must be deleted or the spiritual interpretation and the inspiration that comes with it will be lost.

Our limited knowledge of matter and its energy is not mind or intelligence, it doesn't coexist with Mind. Spiritual knowledge is what we want and it is gained through spiritual sense.

There will be turbulences as the evidence of spiritual sense conflicts with the testimony of physical sense, but the storms will roll away and reveal peace.

The supremacy of Spirit entitles us to antidote the chaotic existence of relativity with Truth and Love. We establish the divine Being and its rule by demonstration, by destroying the imaginary partnership between matter and the eternal Mind. Where is unity found? Where is infinite meaning found? In the Being of infinite Mind.

We use spiritual sense to glimpse infinite Being. Our spiritual sense must be recognized before Mind can be understood. Spiritual sense is assimilated only as we are humble, credible, and sincere. The spiritual sense can't be gained through dullness and grossness. Jesus said, "Do not give dogs what is holy, and do not throw your pearls before pigs, lest they trample them underfoot and turn to attack you."[43]

Spiritual sense is aware of divine movement, permanence, uncontaminated purpose, integrity, glorious possibilities. Here and now. Honesty, meekness, empathy, and charity have divine authority and play a strong role in spiritual healing. This power of healing isn't a supernatural gift, but a skill we all can learn and practice.

What we term physical laws or quantum energy are only beliefs in human mind. Human knowledge has never made us whole, harmonious, or immortal. Human knowledge evolves because it is never completely developed.

Material existence loses its foothold every time physical theories are modified and we overcome limitations. God never ordained a material law. These undeveloped laws and beliefs, along with their merchandise, constitute the flesh. If sin makes sinners, Truth and Love alone can unmake them.

Matter has no life to lose, and Spirit never dies. All substance, intelligence, wisdom, being, immortality, cause, and effect belong to God. No wisdom but Mind's wisdom is wise; no good but God's is good;

---

[43] Matt. 7:6

no truth is true; no love is lovely; no life is Life but the divine.

Real consciousness is cognizant only of the things of God. The realm of real Being is Spirit. As we understand Spirit, our false beliefs are uncovered and primed to self-destruct in the presence of the unerring, immutable, and infinite Mind.

The one Mind is infinite individuality, multiplying ideas of beauty and harmony through us. Mind is the source of all movement and there is no involuntary, unplanned, reactionary, or stopped movement.

Truth is Mind's intelligence, while comparative data is the so-called intelligence of human mind, sometimes clever, always erroneous.

The only death is the death of error. No final judgment awaits us. The judgment day of wisdom comes thought by thought, by which human beings are deprived of all erroneous thoughts. As for spiritual error there is none.

Heaven is not a locality, but a divine state of Mind, where we are found possessing the mind of Love and Truth.

The manifestations of evil which counterfeit divine justice, conjure the picture of an angry God. "And in anger and wrath I will execute vengeance on the nations that did not obey."[44] Correctly interpreted, the Bible verse shows that catastrophes, famines, and plagues are the self-destruction of error, not the destruction of God's children. We have the ability (matter doesn't) to demonstrate the strength and permanency of Spirit We can witness the brightening light of Truth, harmony, and the entireness of God.

Spiritual enlightenment corrects the mistakes that says there is pleasure in intoxication, promiscuity, or wasteful indulgences. Spirituality causes the thief to realize nothing is gained by stealing. The hypocrite sees there is no hiding.

Spiritual enlightenment shows us God created us. We aren't self-made or made by mortals. We are spiritual, but while working our way out of the temporal human façade, we can be as a window— letting the spiritual light of Truth pass through us. The window is kept clear as we wipe away materialism, fear, and exaggerations.

Human thoughts have their degrees of comparison. Some are better than others. A belief in Truth is better than a belief in error. But to be grounded on rock, the belief must advance with divine logic and revelation. Spiritual progress radiates movement from intuition to hope, to faith, to understanding, to fruition, and then reality.

---

[44] Micah 5:15

71

Angels guide. Angels surround us. Angels are pure thoughts from God.

Consider these factors:
- The temporal never touches the eternal;
- The changeable never touches the unchangeable;
- The inharmonious never touches the harmonious;
- The self-destructive never touches the self-existent.

Reproduction by Spirit's individual ideas is but the reflection of the creative power, God.

Without the image and likeness of Mind, God would be a nonentity, Mind unexpressed. But we are Mind's witness. We are proof of Mind, Life.

Truth has no beginning. We can hear Truth, just as prophets did, and still do, even in the middle of a fight with error. As we struggle to conquer false beliefs, we can trust the presence of angel messages to give us spiritual strength and divine power.

God will sustain us under all circumstances. When Moses was called upon to lead the children of Israel out of Egypt, he despaired over making the people understand what God would reveal to him.

Moses was told by the Lord to throw down his staff. It became a serpent and Moses ran from it.[45] Wisdom bid him return, take up the serpent and realize its alarming power was harmless.

Moses was then led to put his hand inside his cloak. When he drew it out, the hand was leprous like snow.[46] He repeated the same simple process and when taking his hand again out from under the cloak, it was healthy. The power of Mind then became Moses' reality and his fear diminished somewhat. Though inspired to help humanity, Moses struggled mentally. He believed his lack of eloquence would be a detriment to the mission. Therefore, God led him to recruit his brother, Aaron, a fluent speaker, for assistance.

Through the wholesome chastisements of Love, we're helped onward in the march toward righteousness, peace, and purity—the landmarks of Being. Be glad to leave behind the false landmarks of human status-quos, judgements, and relativity. In order to continue forward movement, we must put into practice the spiritual good we already know. The one unused talent decays and is lost.

There is no hypocrisy in Being. Integrity is imperative. Human resistance to true new ideas weakens as we give up error for Truth. Our purpose is to live and be like God, Love.

---

[45] Exodus 4:3
[46] Exodus 4:6-7

Here is a list of essential factors useful in the thought process:

1. God is infinite, the only Life, substance, Spirit, or Soul. Truth is the only intelligence of the universe, including person. God and spiritual being are not tactile to the physical senses.

2. Spirit is divine Principle and Principle is not a mixture of good and bad. Principle is Mind, and there is one Mind.

3. The notion that bad is real, is a delusion annihilated by the understanding of good. The effects of that which is bad—lust, dishonesty, selfishness, envy, hypocrisy, slander, hate, theft, adultery, murder, dementia, insanity, inanity—are tied to hell or devils, ultimately shown to be unreal in light of the reality of good.

4. God is unconfined to the forms that reflect Spirit and Love. God is not absorbed. There is no beginning or end to God, Life.

5. All that possesses reality and existence is of divine Mind and Mind's ideas. God is All-in-all.

6. The universal cause is self-existent, filling all space. Spirit is all-inclusive and is reflected by spirituality.

7. Life, Truth, Love are the same in substance, but multiform in office. God is Father-Mother; Christ, Truth, is the spiritual idea of our relationship to God; and the Holy Spirit unites us.

8. The relationship between Father-Mother God and us is tender, yet mighty and complete.

9. Christ is not a human, but the spiritual idea that advances thought toward real Being. It is God speaking to consciousness, dispelling illusions and bringing healing.

10. Jesus was a human being. He manifested Christ and solved the problem of spiritual Being. He showed that spiritual ideas reveal Life, Love, Truth.

11. Humanity can understand the Messiah's example and express Christ, Truth.

12. The word Christ is not a synonym for Jesus, but a title. Christ is synonymous with Messiah, God with us. We can accept, illustrate, and embody God with us.

13. The advent of Jesus of Nazareth marked the first century of the Christian era, but Christ is without a beginning or end. Many people, throughout time, have received, in some measure of power and grace, the Christ, Truth. The divine image is expressed in all generations. Scripture refers to this unity in Jesus' statements: "Before Abraham was, I am," (John 8:58) meaning the human being is not eternal, but the divine idea (Christ) was and is. "I and the Father are one," (John 10:30) meaning our spiritual identity has its being in God, Father-Mother. And, "The Father is greater than I," (John 14:28) meaning God is infinitely greater than the flesh.

14. The duality of the unseen and the seen—the spiritual and physical, the Christ and the

flesh—continues until a pure ascension in thought. Through spiritual progress, the human concept, or body, disappears in Mind-science, yet the Christ spirit continues to exist and take away the sins of the world.

15. Truth is undying. "I am the first and the last, and the living one. I died [was not understood], and behold I am alive [understood] forevermore [the divine rule explains me]."[47] This verse explains the eternity of Christ while also referring to the human sense of Jesus crucified.

16. Spirit being God, there can be but one Spirit. There are neither spirits many nor gods many. There is no evil in Spirit. With divine reality, Spirit does not pass through matter to be manifest. God is not dependent on matter.

17. Spirit created spiritual individualities through Mind, not physical energy. "All things were made through him, and without him was not any thing made that was made."[48] Spirit is the only substance, the invisible and indivisible infinite God. That which is spiritual and eternal is substantial. That which is material is temporal and insubstantial.

18. Soul and Spirit are synonymous. Soul is not inside a body or human mind. Spirit has never existed with mortality.

---

[47] Rev. 1:17, 18
[48] John 1:3

19. Reality is spiritual, harmonious, immutable, immortal, divine, eternal. Sin, sickness, and mortality are contradictions of reality.

20. The Ego is deathless, Mind, I Am. Intelligence never passes through the unintelligent. God never enters evil. The divine Ego is reflected in all spiritual individuality, from the lesser to the greater.

21. Immortal person is God's image or idea, the infinite expression of infinite Mind. We coexist with Life, Truth, and Love. Immortal person has never been mortal.

22. God is indivisible. God can't be portioned out. Divine logic and revelation brings to light the fact that God is fully reflected by spiritual offspring.

23. God is individual and personal in a scientific sense, but not in any emotional materialist sense. We have a personal relationship with Love, yet God is the one Person, reflected by us in our own unique way. God is not a person separate from us.

24. The pure in heart see God.

25. The physical senses and sciences can't comprehend God, Love. The temporal world is a poor counterfeit of the invisible eternal universe. Temporal things are only thoughts of mortals and they disappear in the presence of the spiritual and eternal.

26. Sickness, sin, and destruction can yield to the laws of health and holiness while working out the divine rule. We do not originate in

matter and then acquire spirit. We are not both spiritual and flesh.

27. In the process of divine metaphysics errors of thought can be detected and dismissed.

28. The divine method of spiritual discovery includes destroying vice and wrongdoing. Life destroys death, Truth destroys error, and Love destroys hate.

29. Evil is not the product of God. A sinner can receive no encouragement from the fact that the spiritual rule demonstrates the unreality of evil, for the sinner would make a reality of sin. A materialist can receive no encouragement from the fact that spiritual reality demonstrates the unreality of that which is temporal and unstable, for the materialist would make a reality of the temporal. Materialist thinking, no matter how exciting, is a conspiracy against spiritual selfhood. Outgrown thought processes must be changed, otherwise "You are storing up wrath for yourself on the day of wrath when God's righteous judgment will be revealed."[49]

30. Superstition yields to Truth. Material theories will continue to yield to spiritual ideas as the finite gives place to the infinite, sickness to health, and sin to holiness. You conquer error by denying its reality. The basis of spiritual Being is the great fact that God is the only Mind; and this Mind must be not merely believed, but it must be understood. The materialist thinking will not lose its imaginary

---

[49] Rom. 2:5

power for good or evil until we lose our faith in it and make life its own proof of harmony and God.

The first commandment demonstrates the law of divine Being. "You shall have no other gods before me."[50] All people have one Mind, one Spirit. One infinite God, good, unifies people and nations, constitutes goodwill, ends wars, and fulfills the Scripture, "Love your neighbor as yourself."[51] The law of Truth annihilates idolatry and improves social, civil, criminal, political, and religious codes. Spiritual metaphysics equalizes the sexes, annuls curses, and leaves nothing that can sin, suffer, be punished or destroyed.

---

[50] Ex. 20:3; Deuteronomy 5:6
[51] Lev. 19:18, Mark 12:31, Luke 10:27, Rom. 13:9

Critics Answered

The teachings in this book support systematic mental healing with divine Mind, God. The method can be confused with methods involving human mind powers, thereby inviting undue criticism, however, divine Mind is distinct from human mind.

It is but just to remember that human minds are fallible and their medicines are uncertain sciences. It is fair to say that some metaphysical practitioners, who profess to utilize this divine Mind mental system, don't follow its spiritual rules and in turn become mal-practitioners.

The facts should be kept clear. God helps humanity through systematic divine metaphysics based on mental rules and laws. God's law is a force that sustains and interprets harmony.

Those who raise objections to the law of God and its application to healing, should learn that in the mental system talked about in this book, the factors of superstition, dogma, and opinions are unacceptable.

Intellect, insight, attention to the whole, attention to detail, intuition, and proactive listening are mandatory. These attributes are also effective in the medical field and sciences. Though healing practitioners may not agree in method, many practitioners are aware that they need more than empirical data or emotionally biased knowledge before passing judgment on healing.

Clinical algorithms can be unreliable and misdiagnoses are probable. The use of evidence-based medicines can backfire because statistics embody averages, not individuals. To criticize or censor, by detaching individual cases from the whole, undermines truth as much as criticizing or censoring this book by detaching sentences or phrases from their context.

Denigrations of this book invent contradictions and bury the truths that elevate us from a theoretical to a practical improvement, from materiality to spirituality.

We must be able to perceive the difference between Truth's idea and poor humanity. The sinning race of Adam is not God's creation. We weren't destined to manhandle the world and become superior beings, although this principle enrages the human ego and is the main reason critics aim their indignation toward the healing force of spirituality.

It isn't the purpose of spirituality to make one's own reality. It isn't the purpose of spirituality to prove secular methods are inferior. It isn't the purpose of divine metaphysics to conform to a particular way of life, such as avoiding junk food, avoiding medicine, avoiding sex, or avoiding mean people. To avoid doctors and drugs is the same as automatically dashing to doctors for every scratch and bump or taking drugs as if they are food. Neither standpoint is a means for reaching health, happiness, and spirituality.

Participants in the force of divine Mind realize the normalcy of healthy mindfulness and lifestyles, but to think those elements drive spiritualty and healing is a fateful mistake. The imperative aim of spirituality is to understand Life's ideal and let the divine understanding impel your thoughts and actions as a part of humanity. Our ideal directs our lifestyles, not vice versa.

In the divine interpretation, thought cannot obsess or fixate on lifestyles, symbols, or even a favorite mantra; otherwise you will lose touch with reason and develop a narrow and blurred view of reality— you will make mistakes, errors. Consider a successful math student. The student can't focus on only the rule of addition when working out a problem that also involves subtraction or division.

As for health practitioners, you can't hold fixed notions about a certain diagnosis; otherwise you may ignore information being given by God, or even verbally by the client.

Fixations cause confusion, the penchant to guess, and a lack of mental improvement. We must be receptive to all of the spiritual rules, and they need to be learned and applied in all of life's situations, otherwise the resultant errors will be an unbroken headwind.

Some critics think that students of divine healing are deluded or in some vacuum because metaphysics views matter and its disorders as unreal in Mind. The concept of matter being an error or illusion shouldn't be taken out of perspective in light of the fact that much of the physical reality perceived by humans is not actually true. We are surrounded by mirages and optical illusions. The earth turns rapidly but is motionless to our senses. To deny disease reality isn't to reject truth, but is to accept the truth of Life's ideal, harmony.

Medical theories admit the nothingness of hallucinations, so why condemn divine metaphysics for admitting that all forms of disease are illusions? God does not create or cooperate with disease and sin and we can eliminate from consciousness any notion that painful conditions have a purpose from God.

Reality contains no error; therefore, disbelief in error destroys error and leads to discernment of Truth.

Error is like a dream and when a dream stops it is self-destroyed. Take pain. Many times over, pain disappears as dreams do. It may seem absurd to say pain is an illusion (dream); however, what else could it be? Human beings have forever been at odds when measuring pain levels. The same painful condition to one person isn't even noticed by another person. More bizarre is the fact that pain to one human being is actually pleasure to another. Pain has even been proven to be an error on the physical level. When a supposedly pained human mind is distracted, unconscious, or drugged, where is the pain? Pain is an error, sometimes a terror. Error has no part of Truth and this is an antidote that removes any terror.

Internalized superstitions and a lack of knowledge within your own human framework must be expelled to make room for spiritual understanding. We cannot serve both the human and the divine framework at the same time.

Physical theories do not support life. Matter is not the threshold of Spirit.

Opponents who attack faith should be careful not to confuse spiritual faith with blind faith. Faith is necessary in science, medicine, and religion. Consider the researcher or scientist who is trying to find a cure for cancer; they obviously have faith that a cure exists; otherwise they would not even try.

Metaphysical scientists, also calling themselves Christian Scientists, have faith in God's healing power. Critics of these mental healers, who cannot distinguish between blind (ritualistic) faith and that of spiritual faith can be easily misinformed. Comments and condemnations based on a lack of research obscure any good points being made. Although this book, *from science & religion to God* doesn't obligate you to decline medical intervention, author, Sam Harris, devoted to spreading scientific knowledge and secular values in society, wrote in his book, *The End of Faith*, "If your beliefs are those of a Christian Scientist, obliging you to forgo all medical interventions, you may even have collaborated with God by refusing to give your child antibiotics."[52] The law of Truth and Love, or Christian Science, does not "oblige" any particular human action as if people were androids.

People who insist on proving another method wrong, as if their way were the only way, will end up living out their condemnations. Like the person who adamantly opposes abortion, calling it murder, killing a doctor who performed abortions.

A student of divine metaphysics, or Christian Science, does not collaborate with God as if God were a separate mind. In divine metaphysics, there

---

[52] Harris, Sam. *The End of Faith.* New York: W. W. Norton & Company, 2005.

is no attitude of give-and-take; there is no human element that says, "If you do this, I'll do that." Do physicists collaborate with the law of gravity in order to go to the moon? No. Scientists study the principles of physics, they have the faith those rules will work, they apply the principles, and they go to the moon.

Mental healers study the laws of God, they have the faith those spiritual rules will work, they apply the rules, and they experience Life, Truth, and Love.

It isn't irreverent to stop defending suffering. It isn't irreverent to quit anger-charged condemnations. Physical laws are subordinate to spiritual laws. Answers are found when we are able to collaborate and respect one another.

Spiritual sense must be illuminated and understandably utilized in order to enable one to practice mental healing. The chief difficulty in learning and teaching the divine interpretation accurately is that human languages are inadequate to express spiritual concepts.

Divine Truth is known by its effects, not words. When you do experience spirituality, you may not be able to explain the experience in words that others will understand. Human thought doesn't immediately capture an understanding of the divine equation and its solution. We feel stuck on this material plane, stuck in problems, stuck in words that have multiple meanings. We must educate our thought to the higher meaning where substance is understood to be Spirit.

Instead of insisting matter is substance or that spirit is far removed from daily experience, students of God's law learn that Spirit is the only substance and that Spirit can be part of our daily experience. Divine metaphysics enables us to know how Truth dissolves incarnate illusions and heals the sick.

The starting point of prayer is an understandable God and the living, palpitating presence of Truth.

Until the rules of spirituality are gained, prayers can fail to heal and bless. Our prayers are not practical if we take a superficial approach, or if we believe evil is as potent as God, or if we identify persons as devils. It's the sin, not the sinner, that needs dealing with.

To worship effectively and bring out the spiritual, we can't concentrate our thoughts on the material or on mortals.

Sin and sickness are ghosts. Human beings have yet to outlive ghosts. Time, lack, fear, shame, mystery, idols, objects of alarm, materiality, the grave, are ghosts that continue to haunt us. Only as we understand unlimited Mind do these ghosts disappear and allow us to demonstrate the reality of Life.

Does evil proceed from good? Does good proceed from evil? It is better to employ a truthful health-care practitioner rather than an untruthful prayer that trusts human mind more than divine Mind, Spirit.

Does God create a material human out of Spirit? Does divine Mind commit fraud by making man and woman free to do wrong? Does God then stand on the sidelines waiting to reward the pious and punish the wrongdoer? Would anyone call it wise and good for God to create people and then condemn them to remain servants? Did God create human beings and challenge them to take control of, and dominate creation? No. No. No. No. No.

Truth creates neither a lie, a capacity to lie, nor a liar. If God did create a wrongdoer, a liar, or sickness, we shouldn't be trying to change God's work. But we have a hope that leads us to Truth.

Even if we believe the physical senses are necessary for our existence, hope shows us that we still can change the human concept of life. Our ideals have changed for the better in the past and it can continue. If not, we can start now with a better ideal. We can know Spirit. We can know our self spiritually and practically and act on the higher ideal. We can detect the evidence of the reality of Spirit through our spiritual senses.

You bring out your own ideal. Is the ideal condemning or condemned? Is it mentoring or mentored? Is it war or peace? Is it Spirit or matter? Is your model Love or hate? Is it eternal or temporal? You can't have two models.

No one understands everything and we all learn in different ways. Science and religion can't claim ownership of Truth. Spiritual ideas unfold as we advance. Each idea needs to be correctly identified, put to the test, and developed. The higher hope on earth will always, at first, be rejected and hated until God prepares the mind through divine logic and revelation. The higher hope will be nurtured and will bear immortal fruit when understood; consequently, we keep modifying and revising our learning and teaching and practicing.

True healing is to be honored wherever found. Spiritual interpretations of religion and science are to be honored wherever found.

Study Guide

Teachings in this book may seem abstract, but the process is simple and the results are sure if the subject is understood and the spiritual rules are adhered to. This system rests on the comprehension of the nature and essence of Being—on Spirit's essential qualities. It takes time for us to master spirituality. "And we know that for those who love God all things work together for good, for those who are called according to his purpose."[53]

If healing isn't established through prayer, you can be assured that God will still guide you to the proper use of temporary and eternal means. It's a step by step process and, "God is our refuge and strength, a very present help in trouble."[54]

Everyone is privileged to work out their salvation according to their own light. If patients fail to experience the effects of this Mind healing system, they can resort to whatever other system they believe will afford relief.

Do not condemn rashly. Be charitable and kind toward differing forms of religion and medicine, and to those who hold these differing opinions. We can be faithful to the way of truth while following

---

[53] Rom. 8:28
[54] Ps. 46:1

the divine motto, "Do not judge by appearances, but judge with right judgment."[55]

Sickness is neither imaginary nor unreal to the frightened sense of the patient. Sickness is a solid conviction and needs to be dealt with through a right comprehension of the truth of being.

Divine teachings include entire confidence in omnipotent Mind as possessing all-power, however this should not lead to false self-confidence, or blind faith. Don't abuse this system with thoughtless phrases such as, "God made you perfect."

We need to be honest about our level of spiritual understanding and success. Call upon others if you need assistance. Don't try to raise the dead if you haven't yet performed the simpler tasks of forgiving others and feeding the starved.

Spiritual ideas are difficult to learn and teach because the human language is imperfect. The goal is to expel former beliefs from thought until the shadow of old errors no longer darkens the divine principle.

Teaching isn't a matter of adding more information to a mind, but is an unfolding of spirituality.

---

[55] Matthew 7:1; John 7:24

Teachers shine their God-given light enough to expose in students their latent energies and potentials for good.

Teachers must be aware of the dangers of teaching indiscriminately. Teachers must regard the morals of the student and not only care about class size or payments. Good must dominate in the thoughts of metaphysical teachers and healers or their demonstrations will be prolonged, risky, or phony.

The goal is to silence human will, quiet fear, and illustrate the unlabored motion of spiritual healing energy. Mental treatment is used to cast out selfish assertions, envy, spiritual unawareness, infatuations, arrogance, hatred and revenge, oftentimes incarnate as disease.

It is imperative to be honest. Not human clichés, but divine attitudes reflect the spiritual light and might that heals the sick. Covering iniquity will prevent prosperity and the ultimate triumph of any cause. If teacher or student is ignorant of the error to be eradicated, oftentimes the error turns on and abuses them.

In the spiritual equation there is no authority to trespass on another person's individual right of self-government. There is no authority to attempt to influence the thoughts of others, except it be to benefit them. Never forget that mistaken human opinions, conflicting self-delusions, and reckless attempts to do good may render you incapable of knowing or judging accurately the need of your fellow human.

The rules to remember are to heal the sick when called upon and save the victims of the mental assassins. Mental assassins are those who profess a good God but abuse spiritual truths to suit their own personal agendas. Mal-practitioners try to preserve materialism and status quos while attempting to hide their iniquities. They associate with self-deception, idolatry, elusiveness, and false charity, all of which can't ultimately hide the evil that needs to be destroyed or guarded against. Evil will self-destruct in time.

Beware of the masquerader of this spiritual method. The misunderstanding that thanks God there is no evil and yet serves evil in the name of good is malpractice.

Divine teachings reveal mental malpractice as that which is motivated by malice or by the belief that substance and intelligence are in matter. Don't be afraid of malpractice. We can fearlessly learn that malpractice blasts moral sense, health, and the human life. We can learn how to firewall our thoughts against mental malpractice—a task not difficult when we see that evil can be overcome.

We can learn to expose and denounce the claims of evil and disease in all their forms, while at the same time realizing there is no eternal reality in them. To put down sin, you must detect the sin, remove its mask, and point out the illusion. The sick are healed not merely by declaring there is no sickness, but by knowing health so well that health replaces the sickness as light replaces darkness.

Recuperation is mentally sustained by Truth and goes on naturally.

Sinners are afraid to throw the first stone. A teacher may say sin is unreal, but unless he or she is demonstrating it, find another spiritual teacher. It's a moral offense to indulge in sin, no matter how devout it looks. To say there is no evil is an evil itself until the evil is destroyed.

To talk the right and live the wrong is foolish deceit, doing one's self the most harm. The impure are at peace with the impure. Virtue is a rebuke to vice.

Don't be confused. It will seem as though right and wrong are ever at strife in the mind, but victory rests on the side of invincible truth. We uncover backward thinking, not to injure humanity, but to destroy destructive thoughts.

There is no benefit to injuring others; you will only hurt yourself. We need to practice the good we know in order to advance spiritually. It's more difficult to teach this method accurately than it is to heal the most difficult case.

When Truth is explained, sometimes the hearer's mind reacts. The hearer can either win a higher basis, or return to its morbid moral and physical conditions.

Some people respond slowly to the touch of Truth. Few yield without a struggle and many are reluctant to admit they have yielded to the touch of Truth, but unless they do, evil will boast itself above good.

There are basically three classes of thinkers:

1. The first class oozes with a bigotry and conceit that twists every fact to suit themselves. Their creed teaches belief in a mysterious, supernatural God, and a natural, all-powerful devil.
2. The second class, even more unfortunate, are so depraved that they appear to be innocent. They placidly repeat factoids and incomplete information as if the words are truth, and they never fail to stab their benefactors in the back.
3. The third class of thinkers builds with steel beams. They are honest, generous, noble, and are therefore open to the approach and

95

recognition of Truth. Teaching this mindset is not a chore. Pure thought does not incline longingly to error, whine over the demands of Truth, nor play the traitor for place and power.

Our eyes are pained by the light after we've been walking in the dark. So is it when we've been walking with the world's dark thinking. Don't get lazy and don't fear putting on the new. Outgrowing the old always seem heretical to those who live in the luxury of learning with egotism and vice.

Divine teachings impress us with a high sense of the moral and spiritual qualifications requisite for healing. A grain of spiritual understanding effects wonders, so powerful is Truth, but more understanding must be gained in order to continue in well doing.

Expect to heal by simply repeating words about God, and you will be disappointed. Sin makes deadly thrusts at the spiritual practitioner as ritualism and creed are required to give place to higher law.

Mental states of self-condemnation and guilt are unsuitable and indicate weakness. One must be right themselves in order to walk over the waves of chaotic mortal life, and support their claims by demonstration.

Divine teachings reveal the omnipotence of Truth, which illustrates the powerlessness of falsehoods. To understand, even in a degree, the divine all-power helps rid us of fear. It plants our feet in the path leading to spirituality.

It helps to remember that the higher your attainment in metaphysical healing, the more impossible it will become to intentionally influence humankind adversely.

Teachers need to take care that their student's feeble footsteps are strengthened with follow-up. Continued counsel and loving care confirm the superiority of spiritual power. But remember, that words and mental arguments only assist human beings in bringing thought into accord with the spirit of Truth and Love. God is the real Teacher and we learn spiritually.

Guard against the dangerous quackery of teaching or practicing in the name of Truth, but contrary to its spirit or rules. Adhere strictly to divine Principle and its rules and you will succeed. These rules are not religious or human codes, but instructions or guidelines that expand consciousness out of human limitations and allow the recognition of divine consciousness.

Love for God and humankind is the true incentive in both healing and teaching. Love inspires, illumines, designates, and leads the way. Wait patiently for divine Love to move on the waters of the human mind and form the perfect concept.

Truth does the work and you must both understand and abide by the divine Principle of your demonstration. It requires labor, work, experimentation, and testing to learn and practice the Science of Truth and Love.

Any attempt to heal mortals with human mind is risky and bound to failure. Don't be foolish and think you can gain divine healing knowledge without keeping the facts straight and following spiritual rules.

Reflect the divine law and become a law unto yourself. Wisely shape your course and consistently follow the leadings of divine Mind. You can experience, through living as well as healing and teaching, that Truth is the only way by which human beings recognize a life of goodness, a life of meaning.

Q&A's

The following Q&A's are useful for teaching and learning the law of God, interpreting harmony to the universe, also defined as Christian Science.

Q. What is God?

A. God is divine, supreme, infinite Mind, Spirit, Soul, Principle, Life, Truth, Love.

Q. Are these terms synonymous?

A. They are. They refer to one God and express God's wholeness. God's attributes are good and include justice, mercy, wisdom, honesty, soundness.

Q. Is there more than one God or Principle?

A. No. God is omnipotent, omniscient, and omnipresent Being. God's reflection is person and the universe. The manifestations of God indicate immeasurable Mind, not measurable matter.

Q. What are spirits and souls?

A. To human belief, spirits and souls are personalities made up of contraries: mind and matter, life and death, truth and error, good and bad. Human-made beliefs have tried to divide Spirit, or the one Mind, and the repercussions are idolatry and ritualism.

In divine knowledge, there are not many spirits or souls. There are no contraries in Principle. Spirit or Soul signifies Deity. Spirit can't be rendered in the plural because God is indivisible.

Although human beings are reluctant to admit the unreality of their incomplete concepts of life and substance—called matter—religion and humanity improve from the premise of one Spirit.

Q. What are the requirements to solve the spiritual equation?

A. Don't have many gods. Acknowledge and demonstrate spiritual intelligence, life, substance, truth, and love. Love your neighbor and understand that we all have one Mind, one Parent.

Understand that Soul is not in the body. God is not in person but is reflected by person. Principle is not in its idea. We must reason from cause to effect, beginning with one Mind and ending by attributing all cause and effect to God.

Q. What is the scientific statement of Being?

A. There is no life, truth, intelligence, nor substance in matter. All is infinite Mind and its infinite manifestation, for God is All-in-all. Spirit is immortal Truth, matter is mortal error. Spirit is the real and eternal, matter is the unreal and temporal. Spirit is God, and person is God's image and likeness. Therefore, person is not material, but spiritual.

Q. What is substance?

A. Substance is Truth, Life, Love. Substance is that which is incapable of disorder and decay. God is the only real substance along with Love's expression, spiritual person and the universe. We are substantial as consciousness. Matter isn't substantial.

Q. What is Life?

A. Life is without beginning and without end. Eternity, not time, expresses the thought of Life. What we call matter is unknown to Life in which Spirit is substance. Matter is a human concept that disappears.

Q. What is intelligence?

A. Intelligence is all-power, all-science—or true knowledge—and all-presence. It is the primal and eternal quality of infinite Mind.

Q. What is Mind?

A. Mind is good, God. There can be but one Mind because there is but one God. Having one Mind exterminates the belief in many minds opposing the intelligent, clear, healthy, useful Mind. We can know that God never lapses, never breaks down, and never falls into oblivion.

God remains forever and is our Mind. We can't lose Mind. Our relationship with God is indestructible. We can admit these facts even if they aren't supported by human beliefs. Our spiritual senses can detect our unity with the one Mind and its manifestation of truth.

Q. Are doctrines and creeds a benefit?

A. Zealous adherence to creeds makes it difficult to interpret God as greater than doctrines. Human creeds must give way to spiritual rules that proceed from divine Mind, otherwise progress will be stalled. We follow mindful rules that show God never originated or supported sin, sickness, or death. We act on the truth that God is the only Life, harmonious and eternal.

Q. What is error?

A. Error is a term used to describe human beliefs or incomplete, immature concepts. Error is the contradiction of Truth. It's a lack of understanding. Error is that which seems to be and is not. There is no such thing as erroneous truth.

Q. What about sin?

A. Sin isn't a word to be used loosely. It has more to do with mental conditions rather than human lifestyles or mannerisms. Classify sin as an effect of error, or the mistaken thinking that works against God, Life.

God is sinless and can't create or allow sin. Human beings have a difficult time grasping sinless reality because of the awful fact that unrealities seem real to human beings. God strips off the disguises of sin.

As we better understand God as divine Principle, Love—rather than classify human lifestyles or behaviors as sinful or not—we can establish, by demonstration, the sinless Soul.

Q. What is person?

A. The identity of individuals must be like Spirit, unchangeable good. We aren't made up of ever-changing brain, blood, bones, and other physical elements. Person is idea, the image of perfect Love. Individuals have no mind separate from God. We have not one quality underived from Truth. Person is incapable of sin, sickness, and death. Not one element of error can penetrate spiritual individuality.

A mortal sinner is not God's person or child. Mortal human beings are counterfeits of immortals. Mortals are the children of the one evil that declares we began in dust, as an embryo, or by accident. False declarations are urged to their final limits and self-destroyed. Mortals disappear and we discover we are not fallen children of God, but are upright and loved.

In eternity, person has a complete state of being. When we think of people, we can behold the correct view of the image of God—even when our physical eyes see sinning human beings—and this correct view heals.

Q. What are body and Soul?

A. In reality, our substantial identity is the embodiment of Soul. As we embody Soul, Love, we feel our real body as the reflection of Spirit. Identity is the image of the multifaceted forms of the living Principle. Soul is our substance and never indicates anything inferior to Spirit.

We can glimpse the underlying reality that we reflect Soul in our own individual way.

Q. Does brain think, do nerves feel, and is there intelligence in matter?

A. Human minds, bodies, and matter are temporal, illusive—if Spirit is true. A corpse shows that the brain, nerves, and physical body are nothingness. So, why not now, instead of waiting for death, learn of the substance of divine Mind and act on the somethingness of Spirit?

A connection between intelligence and matter contradicts itself. Matter can't perform the functions of Mind on any consistent level.

We are images of the all-intelligent Mind. It is limited beliefs that make up the brain, nerves, and physical body. Pain and pleasure are not in the human body but in human belief. God is not the author of false beliefs. As we better understand the nothingness of material beliefs their effects disappear. Choose spiritual good as the reality.

Consciousness, as well as action, is controlled by Mind. Harmonious action proceeds from Spirit.

It is backwards to assume the brain and nerves create sin, sickness, and death. It is counterproductive to act as if the brain is powerful, and then try to change it with physical treatments. God doesn't uphold contrary systems and practices.

Assumptions and physical senses may contradict our spiritual identity, however, they do not change the unseen truth which remains forever intact. We belong to God and nothing else.

Q. Do I need to understand the explanations of God's principle in order to heal?

A. Yes. Error will not expel error. Misunderstanding will not eliminate problems. Blind faith will only exchange one problem for another.

To heal spiritually, one must be aware of and obey the spiritual and moral demands. This mental system honors God. The healing work is based on a divine Principle and excludes selfishness, prejudice, and bigotry. Truth must be understood and manifested.

Q. What about medication, hypnotism, theosophy, or psychics?

A. Medication, hypnotism, theosophy, and psychics are human modes of healing grounded in physical laws and human beliefs. Drugs, surgeries, Reiki, massage, channeling, etc., may offer short-term effects, however they are not included in divine healing, in which physical laws and human minds yield to the law of Mind.

The remedial results produced by human modes of healing will be according to what the conscious and unconscious human faith was educated to feel.

Q. Do I need to understand the physical before understanding Spirit and spiritual senses?

A. Physical knowledge can indirectly lead to Spirit and spiritual sense, such as when the computer programmer realizes that mind is outside the machine, or body. We can learn from matter and physics about power, but we won't know the power of Spirit until we understand and make spirituality our experience.

Emerge gently from materiality to spirituality. Don't try to force the subject, but come naturally into Spirit through appropriate knowledge, better health and morals, and spiritual growth. Spirituality is achieved as we exercise Mind-faculties.

As we gain spiritual understanding and learn falsehood's true nature, our spiritual senses are revealed. Earth can be viewed as a preparatory school to learning that Life is deathless.

Q. Who or what believes?

A. Material atoms don't believe. The physical body doesn't believe anything. It's human mind that believes. It believes life is in the body. The believer and belief are one and the same and are mortal.

Spirit is all-knowing. Spirit knows.

The word "belief" can differ from the verb "believe." Beliefs have no foundation if they can't be understood.

Q. Do the physical senses, hormones, and chemicals compose our being?

A. The physical senses, nerves, hormones and so on are only what belief believes. The less power given to material elements, the more readily beliefs go out and we are able to behold the reality of everlasting Life.

It doesn't pay to depend on the physical senses. What the tactile senses tell us isn't the whole story and oftentimes gets it wrong. Why would we go along with the believer who thinks God gave us the tools, or the freewill, to go against God, Mind?

The anomalies in life uncover the falsity of physical sense and bodily influences. There is no reliable matter or universal human law. Human realities and opinions differ. We see they are beliefs without actual foundation or validity. We can change a belief and the sensation changes. We can destroy a belief and the sensation disappears.

Hormones and chemicals are not the medium of Mind. A wrong sense of God and us and creation is non-sense, a want of sense. Even human willpower is a product of belief and can't govern us aright. In divine Science, Truth and Love is the only motive-power of man and woman.

Being is holiness, harmony, immortality. As we understand spiritual being, life is bettered. The understanding requires a war with flesh. Winston Churchill said: "Our task is not only to win the battle—but to win the war."[56] In the fight, physical elements are of no help. New ideas are constantly

---

[56] Churchill, Winston. "Be ye men of valour," BBC Radio, 1940. *Twentieth-Century Speeches,* edited by Brian MacArthur. London: Penguin Books, 1992. Reproduced with permission of Curtis Brown Ltd, London on behalf of The Estate of Winston Churchill. Copyright Winston S. Churchill.

being presented. We outgrow beliefs and Truth triumphs.

All is infinite Mind and Mind's idea.

Q. What is sickness and how is it healed?

A. Sickness and disease are beliefs, experiences of the human mind, fear made manifest on the body. The sensation that we suffer seems real and natural in illusion. The unbroken reality of scientific Being breaks the illusion.

If sickness were true, you could never destroy it and it would be absurd to try.

Choose the immortal over the mortal theory. God will heal the sick whenever we are governed by God. Truth casts out illusions.

Divine Mind must be found superior to all beliefs and fears in order to destroy sickness. We can't doubt the power and willingness of Mind to hold us forever intact and spiritually healthy.

Divine Love always has met and always will meet every human need. Love supplies all good.

We can manifest the infinite ability of Love which in turn demonstrates the inability of sin and sickness. The miracle to grace is not a miracle to Love, but is natural.

When the illusion of sickness tempts you, stick to God and God's idea. Allow only God's likeness to be in your thought. Don't let doubt or fear cloud your spiritual sense and calm trust. Recognize life harmonious. Let divine knowledge instead of physical knowledge support your understanding of being and silence the disorder with harmony.

Q. How can I best progress in the understanding of this system, having been called Christian Science?

A. Study thoroughly the letter and imbibe the spirit. Adhere to the divine Principle and follow God. Learn and show that bad thoughts can't be transferred from one mortal to another. There is one Mind. Your first duty is to obey God, have one Mind, and love another as yourself.

Through God, the Holy Spirit, and God's idea we are enabled to work out the rule of healing, based on Love, underlying, overlying, and encompassing all true being.

Q. Do Christian Scientists have any religious creed?

A. No, not in the sense of doctrinal beliefs. The following six tenets, however are foundational:

> 1. As adherents of Truth, we take the inspired Word of the Bible as our sufficient guide to eternal Life.

2. We acknowledge and respect one supreme and infinite God. We acknowledge Truth, Christ. We acknowledge the Holy Spirit and man and woman as the image and likeness of God.

3. We acknowledge God's forgiveness of sin in the destruction of sin—though sin will be punished until spiritual understanding casts it out as unreal.

4. We acknowledge Jesus' example as confirmation that Love unfolds our unity. We acknowledge that we are delivered to Truth, Life, and Love by healing the sick and overcoming sin.

5. We acknowledge that Jesus' crucifixion and resurrection signify the ability to increase our faith to the understanding of eternal Life, even the allness of Soul, Spirit, and the nothingness of material elements and their phases.

6. We solemnly promise to watch and pray for that Mind to be in us, which was also in Christ Jesus; to do to others as we would have them do to us; and to be merciful, just, and pure.

Interpretation

How we interpret life affects not only our outlook and expectations, but also the consequences. Interpretation is either literal or spiritual.

Taken literally the words, "Clean your room," produces decent results. But when dealing with less concrete concepts, open to wide interpretations, such as, "Be nice," the results can vary. Spirituality comes to our rescue.

Divine interpretation gives us the deeper meaning our hearts yearn for. Spiritual interpretation maintains our life purpose and makes our experiences, words, expressions—even myths— useful. It points the way to non-intrusive healing.

Let's look at a spiritual interpretation of the Bible, starting with Genesis.

Genesis 1: 1: In the beginning, God created the heavens and the earth.

The infinite has no beginning. The word *beginning* is used to mean *the only.* There is but one creator and one creation—God—unfolding.

Genesis 1: 2-4: The earth was without form and void, and darkness was over the face of the deep. And the Spirit of God was hovering over the face of the waters. And God said, "Let there be light," and there was light. And God saw that the light was good. And God separated the light from the darkness.

In this universe of Truth, matter (earth) is unknown. Reality is first presented in light, second in reflection, and third in spiritual forms of beauty and goodness.

Spiritual harmony—the light of ever-present Love illumining the universe—reflects God in countless spiritual forms. There is no element or symbol of disorder or decay.

Genesis 1: 5: God called the light Day, and the darkness he called Night. And there was evening and there was morning, the first day.

Evenings and mornings are used to represent the ongoing appearance of God's ideas. The light represents spiritually clearer views of God. It's revelation, a revealing. The evenings and mornings are not limited to the human concepts of darkness and dawn due to solar light.

Spirit is light. Our current knowledge of reality includes a darkness that suggests an absence of light, but there is no place where God's light is not seen.

Genesis 1: 6: And God said, "Let there be an expanse in the midst of the waters, and let it separate the waters from the waters."

Truth separates spiritual understanding from human knowledge. In spiritual understanding we find divine Mind. We never really find mindless matter.

Genesis 1: 7: And God made the expanse and separated the waters that were under the expanse from the waters that were above the expanse. And it was so.

Spirit imparts understanding. Our spiritual senses grasp the revelations, and the reality of all things is brought to light. Our spirituality helps us know the difference between what is real and what isn't.

Genesis 1: 8: And God called the expanse Heaven. And there was evening and there was morning, the second day.

Spiritual understanding unites with harmony and peace is felt. Each successive stage of progress goes on.

Genesis 1: 9: And God said, "Let the waters under the heavens be gathered together into one place, and let the dry land appear." And it was so.

God gathers and guides unformed thoughts to advance into holy purposes.

Genesis 1: 10: God called the dry land Earth, and the waters that were gathered together he called Seas. And God saw that it was good.

In metaphor, the "dry land" illustrates the absolute formations of Mind—what we call people, animals, mountains. The "waters" symbolize elements of Mind such as compassion, courage, fatherhood, motherhood.

Genesis 1: 11: And God said, "Let the earth sprout vegetation, plants yielding seed, and fruit trees bearing fruit in which is their seed, each according to its kind, on the earth." And it was so.

Mind governs the multiplication of ideas. Creation is ever-appearing from its inexhaustible source. The human mind can't ultimately misinterpret and invert these ideas and call them material.

Genesis 1: 12: The earth brought forth vegetation, plants yielding seed according to their own kinds, and trees bearing fruit in which is their seed, each according to its kind. And God saw that it was good.

Reproduction is spiritual. Gender is mental, not physical. "Kind" isn't confined to the sexual or asexual. The intelligent idea, be it male, female, neutral, or whatever, is designed to indicate the continuity and amplification of infinite Love, not gender.

Genesis 1: 13: And there was evening and there was morning, the third day.

Deathless Life is self-existent, not dependent on material organization. This stage supports resurrection or ascending thought.

Genesis 1: 14: And God said, "Let there be lights in the expanse of the heavens to separate the day from the night. And let them be for signs and for seasons, and for days and years,

This indicates the diffusion and circulation of divine thought as it ascends. The God-centered nature continues to appear. To discern the rhythm of Spirit and to be holy, thought must be purely spiritual.

Genesis 1: 15: and let them be lights in the expanse of the heavens to give light upon the earth." And it was so.

As we turn from the false mortal sense and walk in the light of Truth and Love, we reflect spiritually the illumination of understanding.

Genesis 1: 16–18: And God made the two great lights—the greater light to rule the day and the lesser light to rule the night—and the stars. And God set them in the expanse of the heavens to give light on the earth, to rule over the day and over the night, and to separate the light from the darkness. And God saw that it was good.

Light symbolizes Mind, Life, Truth, and Love. Mind shines by its own light. Mind forms its own images, and radiates their borrowed light. Love rules over hate.

Geology, astrology, and cosmology can't rule, they can't explain the origin and destiny of earth, material bodies, and the stars.

In eternal Mind, there is no darkness.

Genesis 1: 19: And there was evening and there was morning, the fourth day.

God's infinite ideas mark the periods of progress.

Genesis 1: 20: And God said, "Let the waters swarm with swarms of living creatures, and let birds fly above the earth across the expanse of the heavens."

Waters stand for fluid and powerful ideas. Living creatures metaphorically present the progress of intelligence. Birds symbolize high aspirations.

A literal interpretation believes the universe is a mixture of air, solid mass, and liquids, all of which offers limited hope and meaning.

117

Genesis 1: 21: So God created the great sea creatures and every living creature that moves, with which the waters swarm, according to their kinds, and every winged bird according to its kind. And God saw that it was good.

Strength, presence, and power symbolize Spirit. Holy thoughts abound in the spiritual atmosphere of Mind. All natures indicate God's nature, good.

Genesis 1: 22: And God blessed them, saying, "Be fruitful and multiply and fill the waters in the seas, and let birds multiply on the earth."

From infinite Mind comes all form, color, quality, and quantity, and these are mental, not physical.

Genesis 1: 23: And there was evening and there was morning, the fifth day.

Spiritual growth leads to exalted spheres and beings.

The divine universe is dim when we try to control it or measure it physically.

Genesis 1: 24: And God said, "Let the earth bring forth living creatures according to their kinds— livestock and creeping things and beasts of the earth according to their kinds." And it was so.

Spirit diversifies, classifies, and individualizes all thoughts. The intelligence, existence, and continuity of all individuality remain in God, the creative Principle.

Genesis 1: 25: And God made the beasts of the earth according to their kinds and the livestock according to their kinds, and everything that creeps on the ground according to its kind. And God saw that it was good.

God's thoughts are forms of realities. Human thoughts erroneously reverse the order and believe the forms are the reality. For example, moral courage is symbolized by "The Lion of the tribe of Judah."[57] The Lion is not the courage, but a form of courage.

All of God's creatures have access to moral courage. They move in the harmony of divine law. They are harmless, useful, and indestructible.

Genesis 1: 26: Then God said, "Let us make man in our image, after our likeness. And let them have dominion over the fish of the sea and over the birds of the heavens and over the livestock and over all the earth and over every creeping thing that creeps on the earth."

---

[57] Revelation 5:5

The term "man" is used generically here. It encompasses the sons and daughters of God.

God fashions us after the likeness of Life, Truth, and Love. We express liveliness, truthfulness, and loveliness. As the reflection of yourself appears in the mirror, so you, being spiritual, are the reflection of God, Spirit.

Man and woman coexist with God and forever reflect the infinite Father/Mother God.

Genesis 1:27: So God created man in his own image, in the image of God he created him; male and female he created them.

Again, the word "man" signifies the one complete nature of person. Don't confuse the original meaning of the word with the common definition of man as a human male or human being, otherwise it weakens and restricts spiritual power by suggesting a humanlike God, or anthropomorphism.

God is Mind's infinite ideal. Not even eternity can reveal the whole of God, since there is no limit to God's reflection.

Genesis 1:28: And God blessed them. And God said to them, "Be fruitful and multiply and fill the earth and subdue it, and have dominion over the fish of the sea and over the birds of the heavens and over every living thing that moves on the earth."

Divine Love blesses its own ideas and causes them to multiply—to manifest divine power. We are subject only to Life, Truth, and Love.

Genesis 1:29–30: And God said, "Behold, I have given you every plant yielding seed that is on the face of all the earth, and every tree with seed in its fruit. You shall have them for food. And to every beast of the earth and to every bird of the heavens and to everything that creeps on the earth, everything that has the breath of life, I have given every green plant for food." And it was so.

God gives the lesser idea as a link to the greater. The greater always protects the lesser.

Genesis 1: 31: And God saw everything that he had made, and behold, it was very good. And there was evening and there was morning, the sixth day.

Nothing is new to Spirit. Anything original began in eternal Mind.

God is satisfied.

Genesis 2: 1: Thus the heavens and the earth were finished, and all the host of them.

Divine law reveals Spirit and its universe with spiritual beings. We are slow to catch on to Spirit, and only do so as we stop identifying with mortal beings. It's a mental process, requiring constant mindfulness, in which we grasp divine knowledge and identify with Spirit.

Genesis 2: 2: And on the seventh day God finished his work that he had done, and he rested on the seventh day from all his work that he had done.

God rests in action. The ever-active divine Mind is never exhausted, never impoverished. Even from a human standpoint the sweetest rest comes from holy work.

All that is made is the work of God and all is good. God's work is finished.

> Note: According to Bible scholars, in the first chapter of Genesis and the first three verses of the second chapter, God is referred to as Elohim, the mighty. From the fourth verse in chapter two, the creator is called Yahweh, the Lord God. They are two distinct documents.

> We leave the succinct glorious history of spiritual reality and now turn to another creation story—the history of ever-fading mortal realities in which God is not supreme, all-powerful, nor all-present.

> The two distinct accounts of creation allow truth seekers to separate the spiritual from the material or literal interpretation.

The second creation story is a myth. But, a myth we can learn from.

Genesis 2: 4–6: These are the generations of the heavens and the earth when they were created, in the day that the LORD God made the earth and the heavens. When no bush of the field was yet in the land and no small plant of the field had yet sprung up—for the LORD God had not caused it to rain on the land, and there was no man to work the ground, and a mist was going up from the land and was watering the whole face of the ground—

This creation story starts in a fog, a mist that can be confusing. If we didn't know this was a different document, we'd ask: Did God become finite, with a new name, Lord God or Yahweh in the Hebrew? Does God have multiple personalities?

If we do realize this is an alternative account of creation, we ask: Is this creation story the truth, or a lie about God and us? It's a myth, used to teach mortals never to believe a lie.

In reality, Spirit can't evolve its opposite, matter. The divine nature doesn't wing-it as if God is making-up creation without understanding and purpose. God doesn't become part of random human procreation. God doesn't try to satisfy pleasures or gratify senses. God doesn't forget what has been done.

Genesis 2: 7, 9: Then the L𝒪RD God formed the man of dust from the ground and breathed into his nostrils the breath of life, and the man became a living creature…And out of the ground the L𝒪RD God made to spring up every tree that is pleasant to the sight and good for food. The tree of life was in the midst of the garden, and the tree of the knowledge of good and evil.

This creation story now points to Yahweh as blazing a trail to becoming "a man of war."[58] Temptation springs up.

Genesis 2: 15: The L𝒪RD God took the man and put him in the garden of Eden to work it and keep it.

We don't need to cultivate the ever beautiful and complete spiritual realities.

Genesis 2: 16–17: And the L𝒪RD God commanded the man, saying, "You may surely eat of every tree of the garden, but of the tree of the knowledge of good and evil you shall not eat, for in the day that you eat of it you shall surely die."

The myth presents a controlling Yahweh, rather than a self-controlled Elohim and creation.

God doesn't tempt us. Evil does not have the reality of good. Unfortunately, the reality of good is

---

[58] Exodus 15:3

difficult to discern. But, we can escape the unreality by choosing fruit from the tree of life.

Knowledge is helpful; however, spiritual knowledge grounded in divine Life reveals the meaningful experience. Don't ignore human knowledge. Displace it with better and spiritual knowledge.

Genesis 2: 19: Now out of the ground the LORD God had formed every beast of the field and every bird of the heavens and brought them to the man to see what he would call them. And whatever the man called every living creature, that was its name.

Why would God recreate things anew? From inert ground? It's impossible to define something from nothing.

God doesn't need help knowing all creatures by name.

Genesis 2: 21–22: So the LORD God caused a deep sleep to fall upon the man, and while he slept took one of his ribs and closed up its place with flesh. And the rib that the LORD God had taken from the man he made into a woman and brought her to the man.

This record of sleep or hypnosis mocks ever-aware Mind and shows pro-creation beginning with darkness, not light. The result was called woman. Adam never wakes up and woman becomes necessary later to assist in the birth of mortals. This interpretation of existence is fast losing insight and any idea of immortality.

We belong to no lesser parent than divine Spirit, Love.

Genesis 3: 1–5: Now the serpent was more crafty than any other beast of the field that the LORD God had made. He said to the woman, "Did God actually say, 'You shall not eat of any tree in the garden'?" And the woman said to the serpent, "We may eat of the fruit of the trees in the garden, but God said, 'You shall not eat of the fruit of the tree that is in the midst of the garden, neither shall you touch it, lest you die.'" But the serpent said to the woman, "You will not surely die. For God knows that when you eat of it your eyes will be opened, and you will be like God, knowing good and evil."

Now we have a talking serpent, a troublemaker. We can call the serpent the human ego, the devil, the physical senses, bad reasoning, but, this lying creature came to consciousness with a whopping lie, saying—you won't die if you disobey God, Life. But, Mind didn't develop senseless material creatures that dupe others or are easily duped.

Genesis 3: 9-10: But the LORD God called to the man and said to him, "Where are you?" And he said, "I heard the sound of you in the garden, and I was afraid, because I was naked, and I hid myself."

The spiritual interpretation is asking: What are you doing? Why are you looking for happiness in the world? Why are you looking for life and truth in material goods and evils? Why are you still dreaming? Why don't you awake to Love, Mind?

When we don't wake to Spirit, the dream narrative shows how fear and shame immobilize the human mind and cause it to hide.

Did the man and woman of God's creation lose the rich inheritance of Elohim? No. What's more, the spiritual inheritance was never bestowed on changeable human beings. We are spiritual.

Genesis 3: 11–12: He said, "Who told you that you were naked? Have you eaten of the tree of which I commanded you not to eat?" The man said, "The woman whom you gave to be with me, she gave me fruit of the tree, and I ate."

Here is the attempt to trace mistakes back to God. Whether directly or indirectly, mortal human beings do not want to take responsibility for their own thoughts and actions. The woman is the first to confess her fault; she said, "The serpent deceived

127

me, and I ate."[59] This shows that we can learn to distinguish between the material and the spiritual. We can forsake the material theories and go on to discern and experience spiritual creation. We can wake up to Spirit.

Genesis 3: 14–15: The LORD God said to the serpent, "Because you have done this, cursed are you above all livestock and above all beasts of the field; on your belly you shall go, and dust you shall eat all the days of your life. I will put enmity between you and the woman, and between your offspring and her offspring; he shall bruise your head, and you shall bruise his heel."

This prophecy has been fulfilled. The consciousness that Spirit is our origin is available to us. The spiritual idea has given the consciousness a foothold in the divine law that interprets harmony. We have the tools to divide material energy from spiritual energy and experience the heavenly.

Genesis 3: 16: To the woman he said, "I will surely multiply your pain in childbearing; in pain you shall bring forth children. Your desire shall be for your husband, and he shall rule over you."

The task of producing something from something, say, wisdom from Mind, will nullify the traditional

---

[59] Genesis 3:13

128

thinking that something comes from nothing. The belief in something from nothing must go down. Idolatry is doomed.

We can pass through the open gate of divine law into our spiritual heritage.

Genesis 3: 17–19: And to Adam he said, "Because you have listened to the voice of your wife and have eaten of the tree of which I commanded you, 'You shall not eat of it,' cursed is the ground because of you; in pain you shall eat of it all the days of your life; thorns and thistles it shall bring forth for you; and you shall eat the plants of the field. By the sweat of your face you shall eat bread, till you return to the ground, for out of it you were taken; for you are dust, and to dust you shall return."

This human way of life can be awful to contemplate. Mortal existence can be the drudgery of pro-creating without love or building up false images rather than being an image of Spirit. Though mortal existence can be fun sometimes, it's the blind leading the blind. Our passions and appetites end in pain. Superficial joys cheat us. Our gratifications get prickly. Then we die.

What do we gain through toil, struggle, and sorrow? We can gain the strength to bury our beliefs of perishable life and happiness, and reach for the immortal.

***Genesis 3: 22–24*:** Then the LORD God said,
"Behold, the man has become like one of us in
knowing good and evil. Now, lest he reach out his
hand and take also of the tree of life and eat, and
live forever—" therefore the LORD God sent him
out from the garden of Eden to work the ground
from which he was taken. He drove out the man,
and at the east of the garden of Eden he placed the
cherubim and a flaming sword that turned every
way to guard the way to the tree of life.

Unspiritual knowledge excludes itself from
harmony. Sin is its own punishment. Human
knowledge tills its own barren soil and buries itself.

This second creation story is disheartening when
taken literally. The literal meaning implies that God
became like human beings, making mistakes,
reacting without thinking, withholding good, and
always giving ultimatums. Even the opportunity to
reform is made difficult.

A spiritual meaning of the story, however, can be
discovered. The spiritual interpretation regards the
flaming sword as a sword of Truth, with the ability
to drive error out of all selfhood. We can use this
sword to find our spiritual selfhood. The tree of life
depicts eternal reality or being. It's unlike the
knowledge of good and evil tree, which typifies
unreality.

Genesis 4: 1: Now Adam knew Eve his wife, and she conceived and bore Cain, saying, "I have gotten a man with the help of the LORD."

We are reminded not to make the mistake of thinking mortals came from God. Material bodies can't give or take away our immortality. We can learn that we don't lapse into sin, sickness, and death. We can see that Spirit can't create a wicked or physical person. We can know spiritual offspring.

Recognizing the spiritual sometimes causes a mental reaction, generally because it uncovers false beliefs and their effects, but God did not aggravate or bring an evil upon us. The mental reaction is in the human mind and can be calmed by Truth, Christ.

Genesis 4: 3–5: In the course of time Cain brought to the LORD an offering of the fruit of the ground, and Abel also brought of the firstborn of his flock and of their fat portions. And the LORD had regard for Abel and his offering, but for Cain and his offering he had no regard. So Cain was very angry, and his face fell.

Cain represents the mortal conceived without mindfulness, and raised in a world of chance and personal agendas. Cain offers material things to God.

Abel typified the person of Truth and Love, offering a living breathing gift from the heart and mind.

Cain's human literal sense of Love can't help but be jealous, but he doesn't stop to change his attitude, ways, and means. Cain asserts them.

Genesis 4: 8: Cain spoke to Abel his brother. And when they were in the field, Cain rose up against his brother Abel and killed him.

The erroneous belief that life, substance, and intelligence can be material rips apart brotherhood and sisterhood.

Genesis 4: 9: Then the LORD said to Cain, "Where is Abel your brother?" He said, "I do not know; am I my brother's keeper?"

Speaking like the serpent, the troublemaker now takes on a new form and Cain rejects the humaneness of humanity. This denial of truth perpetuates sin, invokes crime, jeopardizes self-control, and mocks divine mercy. It kills spiritual leaders, even Jesus.

Genesis 4: 10–11: And the LORD said, "What have you done? The voice of your brother's blood is crying to me from the ground. And now you are cursed from the ground, which has opened its mouth to receive your brother's blood from your hand."

Though the serpent hides behind a lie and excuses guilt, it can't be forever hidden. Truth, through her eternal laws, unveils error. Truth causes sin to betray itself. Even the habit of excusing irresponsibility is punished. Justice can't be avoided.

Genesis 4: 13-15: Cain said to the LORD, "My punishment is greater than I can bear. Behold, you have driven me today away from the ground, and from your face I shall be hidden. I shall be a fugitive and a wanderer on the earth, and whoever finds me will kill me." Then the LORD said to him, "Not so! If anyone kills Cain, vengeance shall be taken on him sevenfold." And the LORD put a mark on Cain, lest any who found him should attack him.

Justice marks the sinner and teaches human beings not to remove the waymarks of God. When Jesus was being seized and a disciple drew his sword to defend him, Jesus said, "Put your sword back into its place. For all who take the sword will perish by the sword."

Envy's own hell will receive its full penalty, both for what it is and for what it does.

Genesis 4: 16: Then Cain went away from the presence of the LORD and settled in the land of Nod, east of Eden.

The limited human mind falls back on itself. Its erroneous thinking reaches a climax of suffering and yields to Truth by returning to dust, but it is only the sinful nature, not the reality of the person that falls.

The image of Spirit can't be eradicated. The true image becomes more beautifully apparent at error's demise.

In the divine equation we must remember that the physical senses are incapable of cognizing Spirit. Limited personal senses can't come into the presence of God, but dwell in dreamland.

Act on the rule that mortal life, with all its sins and sickness is an illusion, and you can live Spirit and its health.

Does matter support life? Or does Mind support life? Does our mortal history make a significant difference in life? Or does our spiritual history lead to understanding and meaning? Are we material personalities that can be picked apart, subject to psychobabble? Or are we the consciousness of Spirt?

No mortal human mind has the might or right or wisdom to create or destroy.

The fundamental errors of a chaotic and a mysterious material universe taint human doctrines and conclusions. Truth gives us the might, right, and wisdom to recognize and work out the spiritual equation, even demand exaltation.

Scripture appears to contradict itself unless its original meaning is understood. Bear in mind mistakes were made in its transcriptions and translations.

In God's creation ideas are productive, obedient to Mind. Life is self-sustained. Nothing is new to the infinite Mind. We exist because God exists. Paul said, "For as in Adam [error] all die, so also in Christ [Truth] shall all be made alive."[60]

Mind neither produces matter nor does matter produce mind. False teachings, troublemakers, and differing human perspectives do not enter or influence Truth. There is no lesser god.

You can work out for yourself the rule of healing.

While removing from the healing equation any notion that sin, sickness, and disorder exists in Mind, do not ignore problems or physicality. Learn to interpret them properly and sensibly correct the situations with truth.

Although spiritual development has nothing to do with physical theories, we can consider theories of a

---

[60] I Corinthians 15:22

Big Bang, evolution, human creationism, or quantum energy and get hints of an infinite, although they lack a final understanding.

Theories often point to an infinite, an infinite that can be discerned mentally. Spiritual interpretation helps lift humanity out of the limitations of disease and despair into inspired faith. Error destroys itself while spiritual ideas continue to appear.

God is the Life, or intelligence, that forms and preserves our individuality and identity. The true sense of being and its eternal completion can appear now, even as it will hereafter. Truth fosters the idea of Truth. That which is real is sustained by Spirit.

There is no beginning or end in the divine equation. All is God and God's creation. Knowing that God was his life, Jesus was able to present himself unchanged after the crucifixion.

Giving our attention to spiritual interpretations should move us to new standpoints. The mists of error dissolve in the light of Truth, when God, Mind, spoke and it was done.

Let's now skip through the Bible to the book of Revelation for more practice on spiritual interpretation.

Revelation 10: 1–2: Then I saw another mighty angel coming down from heaven, wrapped in a cloud, with a rainbow over his head, and his face was like the sun, and his legs like pillars of fire. He had a little scroll open in his hand. And he set his right foot on the sea, and his left foot on the land,

The angel prefigures the divine force of God that enables us to know and experience spirituality. Angels are messages from God. At first, the messages are obscure, hard to understand. But when we do understand, even a little bit, we are able to heal by its means.

The open scroll symbolizes openness. It shows that everyone has access to the divine forces. We can hear these inspired messages whether at home, in town, in the desert, or in the hospital. We can understand that the power of Truth gives us power over visible and latent errors.

The messages are ideas, so to speak, like ideas in a book, a script, or a song. We can capture and grasp spiritual ideas to study, experiment with, apply, and test. We will find truthful ideas are allied to transformation.

Don't be surprised and don't be discontented when practicing spiritual ideas. Sometimes the truth is a bitter pill and hard to swallow, let alone digest. But swallow truth we must.

***Revelation 12:1*:** And a great sign appeared in heaven: a woman clothed with the sun, with the moon under her feet, and on her head a crown of twelve stars.

Heaven represents harmony, not a physical place on some unknown dimension. Heaven is a state of mind, a state of understanding Truth and Love. The goal is never reached while we hate our neighbor. We need to assess correctly the highest visible idea, and it may be expressed by someone from a different religion or field of study than our own. It's the message, not the messenger that we heed.

We can notice a coincidence between the divine and the human. The human Jesus embraced divinity. This is divinity embracing us and making it plausible for us to understand spiritual Life and its demonstration.

The "woman clothed with the sun" symbolizes all people. Spiritual light encompasses each individual and we can bear witness to this light.

***Revelation 12: 2*:** She was pregnant and was crying out in birth pains and the agony of giving birth.

The spiritual idea is expectant, fertile. It struggles to deliver the sweet promise.

***Revelation 12: 3*:** And another sign appeared in heaven: behold, a great red dragon, with seven heads and ten horns, and on his heads seven diadems.

In Genesis, the lie began as a crafty serpent speaking in the name of good. Now it's a red dragon, inflamed with war against spirituality. It's the disorder, chaos, and hatred, so popular in the world. It's the many inventions of evil that insist life is mortal, substance is material, and that matter has a power of its own.

Don't stand aghast at the lie. But, don't pretend it's unreal unless you've demonstrated and experienced its unreality.

This lie of lies is ripe for self-destruction.

Now, let's see how the Revelator lifts the veil and exposes the lie. The Revelator spiritually interprets that old serpent, the dragon—holding untiring watch and ready to wound—as nothingness. In the light of God's allness, the embodiment of the lie disappears.

Revelation 12: 4: His tail swept down a third of the stars of heaven and cast them to the earth. And the dragon stood before the woman who was about to give birth, so that when she bore her child he might devour it.

The malicious instinct and morbid curiosity, with intents to kill morally and physically even fellow

139

human beings, is unloosed, in order that the false claim of mind in matter might uncover its own crime of defying infinite, spiritual Mind.

Revelation 12: 5: She gave birth to a male child, one who is to rule all the nations with a rod of iron, but her child was caught up to God and to his throne

The new spiritual idea is kept safe in Mind. This idea of safety is useful, especially when you encounter the grossness in human beings bent on doing everything in their power to destroy the spiritual idea.

Revelation 12: 6: and the woman fled into the wilderness, where she has a place prepared by God, in which she is to be nourished for 1,260 days.

We will be guided triumphantly through the dark ebbing and flowing tides of human fear, through the wilderness, through the trying times. Though we walk wearily, we must make the passage from sense to Soul, from limited to unlimited perceptions.

Don't be confused if the spiritual idea is falsely accused with error's own nature and methods. This standard tactic of the liar charging the innocent with the crime, or blaming God for all ills, is an age-old bad habit that must be conquered.

Revelation 12: 7–8: Now war arose in heaven, Michael and his angels fighting against the dragon.

And the dragon and his angels fought back, but he was defeated, and there was no longer any place for them in heaven.

The holy war is the conflict between flesh and Spirit. It is fought by the angels. Michael's character is spiritual strength. Gabriel has the quieter task of imparting a sense of the ever-presence of ministering Love. These angels deliver us from the depths.

Strong faith and spiritual understanding wrestle and prevail over error, sin, sickness, and death. Truth and Love win because the dragon can't war with them.

Revelation 12: 9: And the great dragon was thrown down, that ancient serpent, who is called the devil and Satan, the deceiver of the whole world—he was thrown down to the earth, and his angels were thrown down with him.

The claim that intelligence is in material knowledge either to benefit or injure us, is pure delusion. Spiritual knowledge, Truth, casts out the ancient serpent and his devil angels.

It is the Lamb slaying the wolf. It is innocence and Truth overcoming lust, hypocrisy, guilt, and error. In the spiritual warfare, the divine method achieves glorious results.

Here, the Revelator takes a turn, to depict the fatal effects of trying to meet error with error, hate with hate, or fear with fear, human knowledge with human mortal knowledge.

Revelation 12: 10–12: And I heard a loud voice in heaven, saying, "Now the salvation and the power and the kingdom of our God and the authority of his Christ have come, for the accuser of our brothers has been thrown down, who accuses them day and night before our God. And they have conquered him by the blood of the Lamb and by the word of their testimony, for they loved not their lives even unto death. Therefore, rejoice, O heavens and you who dwell in them! But woe to you, O earth and sea, for the devil has come down to you in great wrath, because he knows that his time is short!"

Human knowledge knows sickness, chaos, errors, and disorders. Suffering increases until we tackle the task of solving the problem of being by becoming familiar with divine knowledge.

Self-abnegation—by which we lay down all, including human theories, for Truth—is a rule in the divine equation. Every human being, at some period, here or hereafter, must battle with and overcome the mortal belief in a power opposed to God.

As we are conscious of the supremacy of Truth, the nothingness of error is seen.

Revelation 12: 13: And when the dragon saw that he had been thrown down to the earth, he pursued the woman who had given birth to the male child.

Human beings are generally apathetic toward spirituality, though they can't ultimately resist the march of mind and honest investigation. Active thinkers will chain, with fetters of some sort, the growing mysteriousness or occultism of this period.

But watch out because the people in materialist stupors could be shocked into another extreme mood—indignation—and they will falsely accuse. One extreme follows another.

Revelation 12: 15–16: The serpent poured water like a river out of his mouth after the woman, to sweep her away with a flood. But the earth came to the help of the woman, and the earth opened its mouth and swallowed the river that the dragon had poured from his mouth.

Millions of unprejudiced minds—simple seekers for truth—are waiting and watching for rest and drink. Give them a drink of spirituality and don't fear the consequences. If the old dragon sends out a new flood to drown the spiritual idea, it can neither drown your voice nor sink the world into the deep waters of chaos and old night.

In this age, the earth will help; the spiritual idea will be understood. Those ready for the truth you impart will give thanks.

Many are willing to open the eyes of the people to the power of good resident in divine Mind, however we hesitate to point out the evil in human thought. We don't expose evil's hidden mental ways of accomplishing iniquity because people like us better when we tell them their virtues, rather than vices. But error must be laid bare.

Without becoming a pompous critic, it requires the spirit of Love to tell people their faults and so risk their disapproval.

Listen to the people who are telling you of the foe in ambush. Avoid the people who see the danger and don't give warning.

Overcome evil with good. Know who you are and God will supply the wisdom and the occasion for a victory over evil. Clothe yourself with Love so human hatred can't touch you.

The conceit of sin will be rebuked. The sublime grandeur of divine law will outshine sin, sorcery, lust, hypocrisy, envy, and outgrown doctrines and theories. Love will fulfill the rule of the spiritual equation and show Spirit's supremacy.

Revelation 21:1: Then I saw a new heaven and a new earth, for the first heaven and the first earth had passed away, and the sea was no more.

A new heaven and new earth were seen, apparently before the human experience called death. The vision was spiritual, metaphysical, inspired. If the Revelator can see a new heaven and earth, we can.

Through different states and stages, the material perceptions vanish in place of spiritual interpretations. We become conscious here and now of a cessation of sorrow, depression, and pain. This spiritual consciousness is a present possibility.

Revelation 21: 9: Then came one of the seven angels who had the seven bowls full of the seven last plagues and spoke to me, saying, "Come, I will show you the Bride, the wife of the Lamb."

The beauty of this text is that the sum total of human misery, represented by the seven bowls of plagues, has full compensation in the law of Love. The very thought that poured forth hatred and torment brings also the experience that lifts the seer to behold the great temple.

Revelation 21: 22: And I saw no temple in the city, for its temple is the Lord God the Almighty and the Lamb.

The temple isn't a material structure, but is the kingdom of God within reach of consciousness now, revealed by the spiritual idea.

This city of our God has no need of sun for Love is the light and divine Mind is its own interpreter. All who are saved must walk in this light.

With the light of Love, let's now review a spiritual interpretation of Psalm 23.

[Divine Love] is my shepherd; I shall not want.
[Love] makes me lie down in green pastures.
[Love] leads me beside still waters.
[Love] restores my soul.
[Love] leads me in paths of righteousness for his name's sake.
Even though I walk through the valley of the shadow of death, I will fear no evil, for [Love is] with me; [Love's] rod and [Love's] staff, they comfort me.
[Love will] prepare a table before me in the presence of my enemies; you anoint my head with oil; my cup overflows.
Surely goodness and mercy shall follow me all the days of my life, and I shall dwell in the house [the consciousness] of [Love] forever.

Glossary

These are the words of him who is holy and true, who holds the key of David. What he opens no one can shut, and what he shuts no one can open. I know your deeds. See, I have placed before you an open door that no one can shut.[61]

In Christian Science we learn that substituting the spiritual for the material definition of a Scriptural word often elucidates the meaning of the inspired writer. On this account this chapter is added. It contains the metaphysical interpretations and spiritual sense of some Bible terms.

Abel. Attentiveness; self-offering; surrendering to the creator the early fruits of experience.

Abraham. Perseverance; faith in the divine Life and in the eternal Principle of being.

This patriarch illustrated the purpose of Love to create trust in good. Abraham also showed the life-preserving power of spiritual understanding.

Adam. Error; a falsity; the belief in "original sin," sickness, and death; evil; the opposite of good—of God and Soul's existence; a curse; a belief in intelligent matter, finiteness, and mortality; "dust

---

[61] Rev. 3:7–8

you are and to dust you will return;"[62] red earth; nothingness; the first god of mythology; not God's child, who represents the one God and is Spirit's own image and likeness; the opposite of Spirit and spiritual being; that which is not the image and likeness of good, but a changeable belief, opposed to the one Mind, or Spirit; a so-called finite human mind, producing other minds, thereby making "many gods and many lords;"[63] A product of nothing as the mimicry of something; an unreality as opposed to the great reality of spiritual existence and creation; a so-called person, whose origin, substance, and mind are found to oppose God, or Spirit; a perverted image of Spirit; the image and likeness of what God has not created, namely, matter, sin, sickness, and death; the adversary of Truth, termed error; Life's counterfeit, which ends in death; hate; a coup d'état against Spirit's creation by that which is called self-creative matter; mortality; that of which wisdom says, "you will surely die."[64]

The name Adam represents the false supposition that Life is not eternal, but has beginning and end; that the infinite enters the finite, that intelligence passes into non-intelligence, and that Soul dwells in material sense; that immortal Mind results in matter,

---

[62] Gen. 3:19; Ecc. 3:20

[63] I Cor. 8:5

[64] Gen. 2:17

148

and matter in human mind; that the one God and
being entered what Mind expresses and then
disappeared in the atheism of matter.

Adversary. An adversary is one who resists,
denies, or argues, not one who constructs and
sustains reality and Truth. Jesus said of the devil,
"He was a murderer from the beginning . . . he is a
liar and the father of lies."[65] This view of Satan is
confirmed by the name often conferred in Scripture,
the "adversary."

Almighty. All-power; infinity; omnipotence.

Angels. God's thoughts passing to people;
spiritual intuitions, pure and perfect; the inspiration
of goodness, purity, and immortality, counteracting
all evil, brute-like inclinations, and mortality.

Ark. Safety; the idea, or reflection, of Truth,
proved to be as immortal as its Principle; the
understanding of Spirit, destroying belief in matter.

God and spiritual beings coexist and are eternal;
Science shows that the spiritual realities of all
things are created by Soul and exist forever. The ark
indicates temptation overcome and followed by
exaltation.

---

[65] John 8:44

Asher (Jacob's son). Hope and faith; spiritual compensation; the ills of the flesh rebuked.

Babel. Self-destroying error; a kingdom divided against itself, which cannot stand;[66] knowledge of material, mortal life.

As false knowledge accumulates from the evidence gained from the five physical senses, the more confusion and the more certain is the downfall of its structure.

Baptism. Purification by Spirit; submergence in Spirit.

"We have confident *and* hopeful courage and are pleased rather to be away from home out of the body and be at home with the Lord."[67]

Believing. Firmness and constancy. Not the wavering or blind faith of human thoughts, but the perception of spiritual Truth. Mortal thoughts, illusions.

Benjamin (Jacob's son). A physical belief as to life, substance, and mind; human knowledge or human mind devoted to matter; arrogance, envy; fame; illusion; a false belief; error masquerading as

---

[66] Matt. 12:25; Mark 3:24; Luke 11:17
[67] II Cor. 5:8 (Amplified)

the possessor of life, strength, purpose, motivation, and the power to act.

Renewal of affections; self-offering; an improved state of human mind; the introduction of a more spiritual origin; a gleam of the infinite idea of the infinite Principle; a spiritual type; that which comforts, consoles, and supports.

Bride. Purity and innocence, conceiving man and woman in the idea of God; a sense of Soul, which has spiritual happiness and enjoys, but cannot suffer.

Bridegroom. Spiritual understanding; the pure consciousness that God, the divine Principle, creates person as the spiritual image of Father-Mother, and that God is the only original power.

Burial. Corporeality and physical sense put out of sight and hearing; annihilation. Submergence in Spirit; immortality brought to light.

Canaan (the son of Ham). A belief in physical sensuality; the testimony of what is termed material sense; the error that would make humanity mortal and would make human mind a slave to the body.

Children. The spiritual thoughts and representatives of Life, Truth, and Love.

Thinking that the body can be gratified and mortal; counterfeits of being, whose better originals are God's thoughts, not immature, but mature; material suppositions of life, substance, and intelligence, opposed to the Science of being.

Children of Israel. The representatives of Soul, not mortal mind; the offspring of Spirit, who, having wrestled with error, sin, and dead end logic, are governed by divine Science; some of the ideas of God thought of as people, destroying error and healing the sick; Christ's offspring.

Christ. The divine manifestation of God, which comes to the flesh to destroy incarnate error.

Church. The structure of Truth and Love; whatever leans on and progresses from divine Principle.

The Church is that organization which gives proof of its usefulness and is found spiritualizing humanity; which rouses dormant understanding from limited thinking to the understanding of infinite ideas and the demonstration of divine Science, consequently driving out devils, or error, and healing the sick.

Creator. Spirit; Mind; intelligence; the animating divine Principle of all that is real and good; self-existent Life, Truth, and Love; that which is perfect and eternal; the opposite of matter and evil, which have no Principle; God, who made all that was made and could not create a particle or element to oppose unbounded Mind.

Dan (Jacob's son). Hypnotism; alleged human mind controlling human mind; error, working out the designs of error; one belief preying on another.

Day. The illumination of Life; light, the spiritual idea of Truth and Love.

"And there was evening, and there was morning—the first day."[68] The objects of space/time, wave/particle, and temporal impressions disappear in the illumination of spiritual understanding, and Mind measures time according to the good that is revealed. This unfolding of good is God's day, and "there will be no night there."[69]

Death. An illusion, the lie of life in human finite mind; the unreal and untrue; that which is contrary to Life.

Human mind has no life; therefore, it has no real existence. Mind is immortal. The flesh wars against Spirit; human mind worries itself out of one belief only to be captivated by another until every belief of life where Life is not yields to eternal Life. Any

---

[68] Gen. 1:5
[69] Rev. 21:25

material evidence of death is false, for it contradicts the spiritual facts of being.

Devil. Evil; a lie; error; not corporeality or mind; the reverse of Truth; a belief in sin, sickness, and death; the power of suggestion, hypnotism; the lust of the flesh, which cries out: "I am living and intelligent matter. There is more than one mind, for I am mind—a fickle mind, self-made or created by a tribal god and put into the opposite of mind, termed energy, afterward to reproduce a mortal universe, including human beings who are not the image and likeness of Spirit, but images of themselves."

Dove. A symbol of divine Science; purity and peace; hope and faith.

Dust. Nonbeing; the absence of substance, life, or intelligence.

Ears. Not organs of the purported bodily perceptions, but spiritual understanding.

Jesus said, referring to spiritual perception, "Having ears, do you not hear?"[70]

Earth. A sphere; an example of eternity and immortality, without beginning or end.

---

[70] Mark 8:18 (Amplified)

To physical sense, earth is matter; to spiritual sense, it is a compound idea.

Elijah. Prophecy; spiritual evidence contradicting limited perspectives; Christian Science, with which can be discerned the spiritual fact of whatever the material senses behold; the basis of immortality.

"To be sure, Elijah comes and will restore all things."[71]

Error. That which seems to be and is not. See page 102.

Euphrates (river). Divine Science encompassing the universe and humanity; the true idea of God; a type of glory which is to come; metaphysics taking the place of physics; the control of righteousness. The milieu of human belief before it accepts sin, sickness, or death; a human attitude, the only error of which is limitation; finitude; the opposite of infinitude.

Eve. A beginning; mortality; that which does not last forever; a restricted view concerning life, substance, and intelligence in matter; error; the thinking that people began materially instead of spiritually—that people started first from dust, second from a rib, and third from an egg.

---

[71] Matt. 17:11

Evening. Mystification of human thought; weariness of human mind; obscured views; peace and rest.

Expanse (firmament). Spiritual understanding; the scientific line of demarcation between Truth and error, between Spirit and so-called matter.

Eyes. Spiritual discernment—not physical, but mental.

Jesus said, thinking of the outward vision, "Do you have eyes but fail to see?"[72]

Father. Eternal Life; the one Mind; the divine Principle, commonly called God.

Fear. Heat; inflammation; anxiety; spiritual unawareness; error; desire; caution.

Fire. Fear: remorse; lust; hatred; destruction; affliction purifying and elevating humanity.

Flesh. An error or mistake of physical belief; misinterpretation of life, substance, and intelligence; a false impression; a belief that matter has sensation.

---

[72] Mark 8:18

Gad (Jacob's son). Science; spiritual being understood; acceleration toward harmony.

Gethsemane. Patience overcoming misery; the human yielding to the divine; love meeting no response, but still remaining love.

Ghost. An illusion; a belief that mind is outlined and limited; a theory that spirit is finite.

Gihon (river). The rights of woman acknowledged morally, civilly, and socially.

God. The great "I AM;"[73] the all-knowing, all-seeing, all-acting, all-wise, all-loving, and eternal; Principle; Mind; Soul; Spirit; Life; Truth; Love; all substance; intelligence.

Gods. Mythology; the trained reaction to think that life, substance, and intelligence are both mental and material; the hypotheses that matter can be conscious; the rationale that infinite Mind is in finite forms; the various theories that hold mind to be a temporal cognition, existing in brains, nerves, chemicals; supposititious minds going in and out of matter, mistaken and mortal souls; the serpents of error, which say, "You will be like God."[74]

---

[73] Ex. 3:14
[74] Gen. 3:5

God is one God, infinite and perfect, and cannot become finite and imperfect.

Good. God; Spirit; omnipotence; omniscience; omnipresence; omni-action.

Ham (Noah's son). Bodily beliefs; sensuality; slavery; tyranny.

Heart. Human feelings, motives, inclinations, joys, and depressions.

Heaven. Harmony; the rule of one Spirit; government by divine Principle; spirituality; happiness; the atmosphere of Soul.

Hell. Mortal belief; error; lust; regret; hatred; revenge; sin; sickness; death; suffering and self-destruction; self-imposed agony; effects of sin; that which "is shameful or deceitful."[75]

Holy Spirit. Holy Ghost; divine Science; the development of eternal Life, Truth, and Love; that which interprets divine Mind.

Human mind. Mortal mind; nothing claiming to be something, for Mind is immortal; mythology; error generating other errors; a suppositional material perception, alias the belief that sensation is in matter, whereas matter is sensation-less; the

---

[75] Rev. 21:27

unreliable conviction that life, substance, and intelligence are in and of matter/energy; that which contradicts Spirit, and therefore contradicts God, good; a false perception that life has a beginning and therefore an end; the limited knowledge that person is the offspring of human beings; the thinking that there can be more than one creator; idolatry; the subjective states of error; speculative perceptions; that which neither exists in Science nor can be recognized by spiritual sense; sin; sickness; death.

I, or Ego. Divine Principle; Spirit; Soul; incorporeal, unerring, immortal, and eternal Mind.

There is but one I, or Us, but one divine Principle, or Mind, governing all existence; people unchanged forever in their individual characters, even as numbers that never blend with each other, though they are controlled by one Principle. All the objects of God's existence reflect one Mind, and whatever doesn't reflect this one Mind, is illusive and erroneous, even the belief that life, substance, and intelligence are both mental and material.

I Am. God: bodiless and eternal Mind; divine Principle; the only Ego.

In. A term obsolete in Science if used with reference to Spirit or Deity.

Intelligence. Substance; self-existent and eternal Mind; that which is never unconscious or restricted. See page 101.

Issachar (Jacob's son). An embodied belief; the offspring of error; envy; hatred; selfishness; self-will; lust.

Jacob. A human being embracing duplicity, repentance, sensualism. Inspiration; the revelation of Science, in which rigid mortal mindsets yield to the spiritual attitude of Life and Love.

Japhet (Noah's son). A kind of spiritual peace, flowing from the understanding that God is the divine Principle of all existence, and that people are God's idea, the child of Her care.

Jerusalem. Ever-changing human principles and knowledge gained from the physical senses; the arrogance of power and the power of arrogance; sensuality; envy; oppression; tyranny. Home, heaven.

Jesus. The best, physically tangible concept of the divine idea that the human mind can conceive, correcting error and bringing to light our immortality.

Joseph. A human being; a higher sense of Truth rebuking mortal certainties, or error, and showing the immortality and supremacy of Truth; pure affection blessing its enemies.

Judah. Human thinking progressing and disappearing; the spiritual understanding of God and spiritual beings appearing.

Kingdom of Heaven. The rule of harmony in divine Science; the domain of infallible, eternal, and omnipotent Mind; the atmosphere of Spirit, where Soul is supreme.

Knowledge. Evidence acquired from the physical senses; mortality; beliefs and opinions; human theories, doctrines, hypotheses; that which is not divine and is the origin of destruction, health problems, and death; not spiritual Truth and understanding.

Lamb of God. The spiritual idea of Love; unselfish altruism; innocence and purity; sacrifice.

Levi (Jacob's son). A corporeal and sensual belief; human person; denial of the fullness of God's creation; ecclesiastical despotism.

Life. Living love. See page 101.

Lord. In the Hebrew, this term is sometimes employed as a title, which has the inferior sense of master, a hierarchy, or privileged owner. In the Greek, the word *kyrios* almost always has this lower sense, unless specially coupled with the name God. Its higher signification is Supreme Ruler.

Lord God. Yahweh. Jehovah.

This juxtaposed term is not used in the first chapter of Genesis, the record of spiritual existence. It is introduced in the second and following chapters when the spiritual perception of God and of infinity is disappearing, leading to confusion from which follows idolatry, the belief in many gods, or material intelligences, as something that can oppose the one Spirit, or intelligence, named Elohim, or God.

Matter. Mythology; mortality; another name for human mortal mind; illusion; intelligence, substance, and life in non-intelligence and mortality; life resulting in death, and death in life; sensation in the insensitive; mind originating in matter; the reverse of Truth; the contradiction of Spirit; the opposite of God; that of which immortal Mind takes no cognizance; that which human mind sees, feels, hears, tastes, and smells only in belief.

Matter/energy. Material energy; measurable, localized forces; a strata of mortal mind.

Mind. The only I, or Us; the only Spirit, Soul, divine Principle, substance, Life, Truth, Love; the one God; not that which is *in* man and woman, but the divine Principle of whom God's child is the full and perfect expression; Deity, which outlines but is not outlined. See page 101.

Miracle. That which is divinely natural, but must be learned humanly; a phenomenon of Science.

Morning. Light; symbol of Truth; revelation and progress.

Moses. A fleshly human being; moral courage; a type of moral law and the demonstration thereof; the proof that without the gospel—the union of justice and compassion—there is something spiritually lacking, since justice demands penalties under the law.

Mother. God: divine and eternal Principle; Life, Truth, and Love.

New Jerusalem. Divine Science; the spiritual facts and harmony of the universe; the kingdom of heaven, or domain of harmony.

Night. Darkness; doubt, fear.

Noah. A fleshly human being; knowledge of the nothingness of temporal things and of the immortality of all that is spiritual.

Oil. Dedication; altruism; gentleness; prayer; heavenly inspiration.

Person. The compound idea of infinite Spirit; the spiritual image and likeness of God; the full representation of Mind. Man and woman. An individual. See page 103.

Pharisee. Bodily and sensuous belief; self-righteousness; vanity; hypocrisy.

Pishon (river). The love of the good and beautiful, and their spirituality and immortality.

Principle. Origin and outcome. See page 99.

Prophet. A spiritual seer; disappearance of limited perceptions before the conscious facts of spiritual Truth.

Purse. Storing up treasures in material things; error.

Red Dragon. Error; fear; inflammation; sensuality; manipulation; hypnotism; jealousy; revenge.

Resurrection. Spiritualization of thought; a new and higher idea of immortality or spiritual existence; material belief yielding to spiritual understanding.

Reuben (Jacob's son). Corporeality; sensuality; delusion; mortality; error.

River. Channel of thought.

When smooth and unobstructed, it typifies the course of Truth; but muddy, foaming, and dashing, it is a type of error.

Rock. Spiritual foundation; Truth. Aloofness and stubbornness.

Salvation. Life, Truth, and Love understood and demonstrated as supreme over all; sin, sickness, and death destroyed.

Seal. The signet of error revealed by Truth.

Serpent (*nāhāš,* in Hebrew; *ophis,* in Greek). Subtle deceit; a lie; an error that conflicts with Truth; the first affirmation of mythology and idolatry; the belief in more than one God; hypnotism; the first lie of limitation; finiteness; the first claim that there is an opposite of Spirit, good, termed matter or evil; the first delusion that error exists as fact; the first claim that sin, sickness, and death are the realities of life. The first audible claim that God was not omnipotent and that there was another power named evil, which was as real and eternal as God, good.

Sheep. Innocence; inoffensiveness; those who follow their leader.

Shem (Noah's son). A structural, measurable human; kindly affection; love rebuking error; gratification of the flesh reproved.

Sin. Thoughts not based on and aimed toward the one Spirit. Disobedience to, and unawareness of, the one God and our spiritual selfhood.

Son. The Son of God, the Messiah or Christ. The son of human beings, the offspring of the flesh. "Son of a year."

Souls. Human feelings coming and going. See page 99.

Space/time. Empty area; interval; relative position and direction; a beginning and an end.

Spirit. Divine substance; Mind; divine Principle; all that is good; God; only that which is perfect, everlasting, omnipresent, omnipotent, infinite.

Spirits. Human beliefs; physicality; evil minds; supposed intelligences, or gods; the opposites of God; errors; fantasies. See page 99.

Substance. Love. The consciousness of Spirit. See page 100.

Sun. An example of Soul governing man and woman. The symbol of Truth, Life, and Love.

Sword. The idea of Truth; justice; Revenge; anger.

Temple. Body; the idea of Life, substance, and intelligence; the structure of Truth; the sanctuary of Love; a material structure where humanity congregates for worship.

Tenth. Contribution; tithe; showing reverence; gratitude; a sacrifice to the gods.

Thummim. Perfection; the eternal demand of divine Science.

The Urim and Thummim, which were to be on Aaron's breast when he went before Yahweh, were holiness and purification of thought and deed—the mindset that prepares us for the office of spiritual teaching.

Tigris (river). Divine Science understood and acknowledged.

Time. Mortal measurements; limits, in which are summed up all human acts, thoughts, beliefs, opinions, knowledge; matter; error; that which begins before, and continues after, what is termed death, until the mortal disappears and spiritual perfection appears.

Uncleanness. Impure thoughts; error; sin; dirt.

Ungodliness. Opposition to the divine Principle and its spiritual idea.

Unknown. That which spiritual sense comprehends. The unknown is unknown to the physical senses.

Some thinkers may believe God is unknowable, but Christian Science makes God known as the All-in-all, forever near.

Paul saw in Athens an "altar with the inscription, 'To an unknown god,'" and he said to the Athenians: "What therefore you worship as unknown, this I proclaim to you."[76]

Urim. Light.

It was believed that the stones in the breastpiece of the high-priest had supernatural illumination, but divine Science reveals Spirit, not some device, as the illuminator of all. The illuminations of Science give us a sense of the nothingness of error, and they show the spiritual inspiration of Love and Truth to be the only fit preparation for admission to the presence and power of the Most High.

Valley. Depression; humility; darkness.

---

[76] Acts 17:23

"Even though I walk through the valley of the shadow of death, I will fear no evil, for you are with me."[77]

Though the way is dark in mortal sense, divine Life and Love enlighten the way, destroy the restless human thinking, the fear of death, and the supposed reality of error. Christian Science, contradicting the feeling of depression, makes the valley to bud and blossom as the rose.

Veil. A cover; concealment; hiding; hypocrisy.

Veils are worn by women as a sign of reverence. Veils are also ritualistically worn as a mark of submission, in compliance with the notions of religious scholars.

Our motives and inclinations are paramount in religion. However, when rituals and ceremonies are the crux of religion, the motives and inclinations of a person are concealed by formal procedures and human routines. Jesus, as modest as he was mighty, rebuked this hypocrisy. Hypocrisy offers long petitions for blessings on physical rituals, but veils the crime latent in thought, which is ready to spring into action and crucify God's anointed. The martyrdom of Jesus was the culminating sin of Pharisaism. Jesus' action rent the veil of the temple.

[77] Ps. 23:4

It revealed the false foundations and structures of superficial religion, tore from bigotry and superstition their coverings, and opened the tomb with divine Science—immortality and Love.

Weeds. Mortality; error; sin; sickness; disease; death.

Wilderness. Loneliness; doubt; darkness. Spontaneity of thought and idea; the entrance in which a mortal sense of things disappears, and spiritual sense unfolds the great facts of existence.

Will. The motive-power of error; human belief; animalistic power. The might and wisdom of God.

"It is God's will."[78]

Will, as a quality of so-called human mind, is a wrong-doer; therefore, it should not be confused with the term as applied to Mind or to one of God's qualities.

Wind. That which indicates the might of omnipotence and the movements of God's spiritual government, encompassing all things. Destruction; anger; human passions.

The Greek word for wind, *pneuma,* is also used for spirit, as in John's Gospel where we read, "The

---

[78] I Thess. 4:3

wind [*pneuma*] blows wherever it pleases…So it is with everyone born of the Spirit [*pneuma*]."[79] Here the original word is the same in both cases, yet it has received different translations (as have other passages elsewhere in the New Testament). This shows how the Teacher had constantly to employ words that were significant to humanity in order to unfold spiritual thoughts. In the record of Jesus' supposed death, we read: "Jesus breathed his last."[80] Indeed, what Jesus gave up was air, an etherealized form of matter, for he never did give up Spirit, or Soul.

Wine. Inspiration; understanding. Error; fornication; temptation; emotionalism.

Winnowing Fork. Fan; separator of fable from fact; that which gives action to thought.

Year. A solar measurement of time; mortality; space for repentance.

"With the Lord a day is like a thousand years."[81]

One moment of divine consciousness, or the spiritual understanding of Life and Love, is a foretaste of eternity. This exalted view, obtained and retained when the Science of being is

---

[79] John 3:8
[80] Luke 23:46; Mark 15:37
[81] II Peter 3:8

171

understood, would bridge over with life discerned spiritually the interval of death, and humanity would be in the full consciousness of our spirituality and eternal harmony, where sin, sickness, and death are unknown. Time is a human thought, the divisor of which is the solar year. Eternity is God's measurement of Soul-filled years.

You. As applied to a physical body, a mortal human; finitude.

Zeal. The reflected animation of Life, Truth, and Love. Blind enthusiasm; human will.

Zion. Spiritual foundation and structure; inspiration; spiritual strength. Emptiness; unfaithfulness; desolation.

Index

93096112R00104

Made in the USA
Columbia, SC
09 April 2018